AMERICAN LIVES

Series editor:

Tobias Wolff

MY RUBY SLIPPERS

....

The Road Back to Kansas

....

Tracy Seeley

UNIVERSITY OF NEBRASKA PRESS

LINCOLN AND LONDON

Library of Congress Cataloging-in-Publication Data

Seeley, Tracy.
My ruby slippers : the road back to Kansas / Tracy Seeley.
    p. cm. — (American lives)
Includes bibliographical references.
ISBN 978-0-8032-3010-1 (pbk. : alk. paper)
1. Seeley, Tracy—Travel—Kansas. 2. Seeley, Tracy—Childhood and youth. 3. Kansas—Social life and customs. 4. Kansas—Description and travel. 5. Kansas—Biography. 6. Place (Philosophy) I. Title.
CT275.S469A3 2011   978.1092—dc22
    [B]   2010025586

Set in Monotype Dante by Bob Reitz.
Designed by A. Shahan.

For all my relations

[S]trangely aware of some lost land
in herself, she took to going out;
wandering the countryside; . . .
to other cities, alone and engrossed.

DJUNA BARNES
Nightwood

Contents

Prelude

I.

I hear it in the produce aisle amid the baby artichokes, one drag queen to another. At the annual Bay to Breakers 12K race, when centipede teams inside hot dogs or Spanish galleons and runners in costumes or nothing at all run the width of the city, seven-plus miles of mayhem. I hear it at the gay pride parade, or amid the tattooed tribes of the Haight, and at the yearly Halloween bacchanal. A woman dressed as a light bulb crows to her boyfriend the Faerie Queene, the carnival raging around them, "Gee, Toto, I guess we're not in Kansas anymore."

It's the unofficial San Francisco motto. The place even looks like the Emerald City rising from the fog, the tips of its towers glistening, when I drive back home across the Bay Bridge. And every year, when *The Wizard of Oz* plays at the Castro Theater, a thousand boisterous, costumed celebrants cheer for the Cowardly Lion, mouth all the dialogue, and sing every song. There's no place like home? Are you kidding? Nearly everyone I meet here has escaped Kansas or somewhere like it, and no one dreams of going home. Who would give up her sparkling ruby dancing shoes for a farm house in the middle of a desiccated nowhere? We've flown the flyover zone. Our migration has saved us. Reinvented, reeducated, recoiffed, and redeemed, we live fascinating, urbane lives.

Or at least that's what we tell our satisfied selves. Most Kansans are rightly sick of the clichés, Dorothy and Oz and the flyover zone.

I will eventually surprise myself by being sick of them, too. But at the time this book begins, I'd bought into the hype. And then I decided to return.

I grew up in Kansas. But for decades, I didn't want the Kansas taint to touch me. I didn't even name it as the prelude to my tale of escape. When I went away to college in Texas, I quickly learned that in the popular mind, even the Texas popular mind, Kansas was flat, dull, and culturally backward. Texas, like Kansas, has High Plains and desert to the west, piney woods and hills to the east, and lots of nothing in between. Its cultural sophistication was not, let's say, widely touted. But unlike Kansas, it also had panache, a national myth that made it rise above geography and hickdom like a lone, shining star.

Knowing this at eighteen as I had only sensed it before, I worked at shucking Kansas off like the skin of a cicada. I rounded out my nasal vowels and entered academe, a world that stood in no real place but the mind. I finished graduate school and taught at Yale. By the time I arrived in San Francisco in 1993, I had brushed the Kansas dust from my newly fashionable shoes. I had taken on the patina of travel and books and a life in other parts.

By the time this story begins, say 1999, my life had settled into a routine and cultured ease. My two daughters were grown and gone, I lived in a picture-book Victorian with a charismatic man I'll call P, and my morning commute entailed a ten-minute walk through a eucalyptus grove in Golden Gate Park. On non-teaching days, my office was a table in a neighborhood café, in the company of others sipping lattes at two in the afternoon. Three or four nights a week, P and I ate in one of a dozen restaurants whose menus we'd memorized and that we liked to think of as "ours." Almost as often we settled into plush seats in some movie palace or other for the evening's independent film, a visual feast that culminated in the late-April gluttony of a dozen tickets to the International Film Festival. On weekends, we rode our bikes to the beach or hiked the Marin Headlands—where in one direction we could look out at the Golden

Gate Bridge, and in the other, the Pacific—or we headed down the coast for lunch at some out-of-the-way place we'd found in *California Back Roads*. From March to November, we reveled in the morning fog and Mediterranean afternoons, the weather never too hot or too cold; even in so-called winter, flowers always bloom.

In rare, reflective moments in a city of stunning natural beauty, its architecture draped in gingerbread, its attitude draped in wit, it unsettled me that in San Francisco I had joined the land of the lotus eaters, intoxicated by pleasure, forgetful of our pasts in other lands. In those moments, the city seemed to float three inches off the ground, ephemeral and unrooted. Most days, though, I enjoyed the levitation.

Then my parents, long divorced, died in the same year, two weeks apart.

When my mother died, I sank into the deep and uncomplicated grief of a bereft child. But when my father followed, it seemed a perverse and distant afterthought, as though years of estrangement had not, after all, been able to keep him away. It seemed unfair that he should share my mother's untainted threnody. He had already been gone too long. Decades of absence had drained my store of sorrow.

My grief eventually settled like sediment in a pond, stirred up now and then by a birthday or death day or unexpected reminder. What remained was the double blunt reminder of mortality and the shortness of time. And a list of thirteen addresses.

II.

On the end papers of my yellow baby book, my mother, then young, had taped greeting cards covered in ducks and diaper pins, angels and storks, cards from people I didn't know welcoming me to the world. Inside she had recorded my first step, first words, cute sayings, friends' names, and how I'd celebrated my birthdays, one through six. And on the page titled "Addresses," she had written all thirteen: seven addresses in Colorado by the time I was four, six in

Kansas after, all before I turned nine. She'd written them at different times, once for each time we moved, the handwriting growing more hurried and—I imagined—more resigned as she noted another of my father's failures to stay anywhere for long.

In my early twenties, when I pulled the book out of a box, the greeting cards dangled from brittle bits of yellowing tape and the edges of the pages had browned. Inside I found my newborn footprints, as tiny as my new daughter Erin's had been only months before, and photos of my birthdays. Age one, a big-eyed baldy with fat cheeks dipped in chocolate frosting; age six, a smiling girl in a blue flowered dress, cheek coyly leaning on one hand. Clues to the girl I'd been. But the addresses exuded a different kind of charm, suggestive and mysterious. What was that life in Colorado I didn't remember? Why so many addresses? What was Kansas to me? Vaguely thinking I might someday visit them all to see where I had been, I copied the list onto lined yellow paper and filed it under "Family History."

Once time had muted my mother's death, that address list began to stir. Kansas crept into my conversation, and I pondered going home. But where was that exactly? The very idea seemed jittery and jangled. How could I know anything about those places for which I had no stories? Why had Kansas never felt like home?

III.

In an essay on the blind poet Jorge Luis Borges, N. Scott Momaday writes, "Once in his life a man ought to concentrate his mind upon the remembered earth . . . to give himself up to a particular landscape in his experience, to look at it from as many angles as he can, to wonder about it, to dwell upon it. He ought to imagine that he touches it with his hands at every season and listens to the sounds that are made upon it. He ought to recollect the glare of noon and all the colors of the dawn and dusk."

For Momaday the "remembered earth" is the storied earth. It is the earth he recalls in *The Way to Rainy Mountain*, the Kiowa stories of his tribe's journey from Yellowstone to the Black Hills and finally to the Wichita Mountains in Oklahoma. "The journey began one day long ago on the edge of the northern Plains," he begins. I love the article "the" at the start of his story—not *my* journey, but *the* journey. The journey that is larger than himself, larger than his grandmother's memory. It is a story of so many generations that when his grandmother recounts what she knows, "although [she] lived out her long life in the shadow of Rainy Mountain, the immense landscape of the continental interior lay like memory in her blood. She could tell of the Crows, whom she had never seen, and of the Black Hills, where she had never been."

Reading Momaday, I felt impoverished. I had never contemplated my many landscapes so deeply, looking, wondering, touching them in all seasons, listening to their sounds. And I had so few stories. My parents' anecdotes had always been paltry, their storytelling little more than allusions to place names and the shadow of unspoken tales. We had no oral tradition, no stories deeply rooted in soils deeply remembered, no collective journey's telling to remind us of who we were or where we had been.

Now I'd lost my chance to ask my parents for more. But in their dying, I'd also gained the freedom from being their child. I could map our emotional landscapes to the places we had lived, free of their watchful and wary eyes. As I imagined the possibilities, those thirteen addresses took on the power of a spell and became an incantation.

Over the next five years, they would carry me back again and again to Kansas as I filled in the silences of my family's story. I would also begin to learn what else I had been missing. That larger absence first whispered its name to me in the Ute Museum in Montrose, Colorado, in the continuous loop of a video projection. Sitting on a log, surrounded by trees, a Ute elder spoke of what removal from the mountains meant to the tribes. The sorrow of losing an ancestral place, one that molds the very shape of thought, runs like a silver thread through his speech. "When you live in a place for a long time," he says, "you think that way."

Having heard that, I would wonder what it meant. If you've never lived anywhere for long, what is the shape of your thought then? What can place mean?

In August of 2001, more than two years since my mother's funeral, feeling tugged by those questions without yet knowing what they were, I set my departure date for the following June.

IV.

There is the map of the journey and the journey itself, and in the chasm between them, this story begins again. Still in the Victorian house with the charming P, living a postcard life in a city of languorous ease, I again surveyed the fields and streams below me as the sun shone and saw that they were good. Then the earth heaved and rumbled, splitting beneath my feet, and I, no longer borne up by any certainty, felt for a moment suspended and weightless, held aloft by my own suspended breath until, yanked hard by gravity, I plummeted through open and frightening air.

I found a lump. In late October I lay on the couch, as I had lain for weeks, immobilized by the burning, falling towers of the World Trade Center. Staring at endless variations of the same scene, listening to every update devoid of news, I felt enveloped in fog. For weeks I had moved through my days as though struggling through water. In class my students and I delved into the literature of the 1930s. The collective despair and alarm of that decade between wars, in anticipation of wars, with its repressions and calls to arms, left our nerves raw. Flags waved and war drums began to sound, and I felt exiled by my own politics, living in a place that had no place for me. In the evening, watching the towers fall, I lay wrapped in a dull shroud.

On occasion I shifted my weight or adjusted a pillow, just enough to suggest I was still in the room. Idly, absentmindedly, I slid a hand under my sweater one night to check for lumps. No big deal. Routine. And there it was, the size of a marble, round like a marble, and brand new. Hmmm. I rolled it between my fingers, trying to feel unalarmed. I'd had lumps before, all benign. Here was another.

xvi   Prelude

I tried to ignore it and wait for it to disappear, but whenever I dressed or showered and fingered its alien roundness, the marble didn't seem to be going anywhere. It intruded into lectures and poems or suddenly appeared in the middle of a sentence or conversation. It sat in the front of my brain and stared. It shook me awake at night.

Finally, in December I made an appointment for January, after the holidays. Then, I'd find out it was nothing.

Christmas came and went as the gray fog of winter was lit up by electrical storms at home. P twisted and writhed in the throes of a cliché. At midlife, he didn't know what to do with himself. He wanted children. I held my breath. He didn't want children. I exhaled. He wanted to go home to Latin America. He loved America. He hated America. I was American. He was tired of speaking English; he was sick of the States, with its war threats and imperial bluster. He wanted a change. He didn't know what he wanted. He went home for two weeks, to speak his native language and touch his native world.

Meanwhile, my doctor took one look at the lump and filled my appointment book with radiologists and surgeons. P came home still confused. A something showed up on the mammogram, a tangled net of light and shadow. While we waited for the biopsy results I already knew, P kept insisting, "You'll be fine. You'll be fine." As though there were no room in our life for me not to be fine. Or at least no room in his.

On Monday the surgeon said, "It's cancer."

On Tuesday P said, "I'm in love with someone else."

For those two days, for longer, there was nothing but the sound of the solid world splintering and wind roaring through the abyss.

Cancer isn't really the story I've come to tell. Or at least not the only one. Nor is this the tale of P and the Victorian house, which I left a week after my surgery. But those evictions—from a country that felt newly foreign, from a healthy body, from a house and relationship

I'd loved—left me suspended in a nonplace that felt all too familiar. The ghosts of my dozen childhood moves and my father's leaving had laid their chilly hands on my heart.

This time, though, there was also something new. Before Christmas, by coincidence or not, I'd signed up for a class on meditation set to begin in the new year. During the first class meeting, we began by meditating on a raisin.

Close your eyes. Take the raisin in your mouth. . . . Notice the raisin. . . . Feel it with your tongue. . . . Simply notice. . . . Feel the texture, the wrinkles, the bit at the end. Now bite. . . . Notice. Notice the taste, the crinkly outside, the soft wet in, the sweet, the tart, the juices sluicing. . . . Notice the bits that swim and the bits that stick, the feel of your teeth on your tongue, the hardness, the softness, the wet. . . . Taste. . . . Swallow. . . . Notice. . . . Notice the taste on your tongue. . . . Notice. . . . Breathe. . . . Slowly open your eyes.

How was that?

That was the best raisin of my life.

Now live that way. Simply notice. Breathe in, breathe out. Notice your present experience—taste the raisin of the world. Let the rest of it fall away, like a breath. Everything changes, like the raisin; taste what's there, and then breathe out. Taste it, and then let it go.

Over the weeks of meditation practice, my intertwined sorrows of displacement softened. Grief, anger, and fear—each had its moment, but proved fleeting if I would only notice then let it go. My surgeon removed the lump, and I moved to a new apartment. I went through chemo and my hair fell out, and then I moved again—this time evicted by the pounding bass from a club next door that rattled my windows late into the night. For seven weeks I showed up for my daily dose of radiation. Things were what they were; they could not be different. And they, like all things, would pass. Life in San Francisco went on as usual outside my bedroom window. But even as my orbit grew smaller, the world grew large.

People will sometimes tell you that a life-threatening illness is a gift. That's a load of crap. The gift is the strength and humor, endurance and optimism I've seen cancer patients bring to the challenge, even while they are dying. The gift for me while I felt my losses and took my lumps was how I learned to live. Meditation brought me a less-protected, more-open heart and a readiness to see things as they were. It made my trip to Kansas more than a matter of curiosity but a pilgrimage of reconnection. A return to the place I'd come from, unembarrassed to claim it and know it. A journey to touch ground.

A month after I hopped off the radiation table for the last time—my bald head sprouting a fine haze of hair; my body fatigued, burned, and bruised; but my spirits calm and strong—I felt ready to step into that vast in-between. That infinite space between what was past and what was next, like the pause between an in breath and an out. I booked a ticket to Denver, grabbed my thirteen addresses, and took to the road.

....

CHAPTER ONE

Thresholds

The night before crossing the Rockies, I had three dreams. In the first, I was going to teach for the first time, but the semester had already started. I entered my classroom, but someone else was lecturing. Students scribbled in their notebooks. I balked, but I told myself to be humble, let someone else be in charge. The class started a game I didn't know, and the teacher directed students to stand up if they got an answer right, to remain seated if they didn't. Then it was my turn to lead the game, and I told the students to sit on the table instead of standing. But the table was too high, and when several struggled to climb up, they couldn't. I resigned myself to the old rule, standing. Then I couldn't remember the question I'd asked; and since the game built on previous questions and answers, I couldn't go on.

The second dream. Confused, I stood at a dark corner in a watery pool of streetlight. A broad valley sprinkled with lights spread out below me. Its peacefulness only heightened my anxiety. I needed to get somewhere. But where? Near the corner, a woman pulled out of a small garage and backed down a driveway, which was blocked by a gate made of corrugated plastic. I wondered, should I open the gate? Suddenly, I was hiding in the car's backseat. The woman backed the car into the road, and a young, dark-haired man appeared in the front seat beside her. I spoke and they startled. I could feel their fear. I apologized and asked if they would give me a ride, but the woman swerved to the shoulder and told me to get out. The car's taillights disappeared into the dark. I started walking in one direction but panicked, turned back, turned again down another dark street, around another corner. I was inside a brightly lit building, at the top of a short, broad flight of stairs. Light glinted off a wall of handmade tiles—lavender, yellow, and orange—painted with fish and seashells and the shapes of children's hands. In my waking life, I had often walked past that wall at Avila Elementary in San Francisco. But in the dream, I was in the Mission Cultural Center, relieved to be somewhere I knew. I stepped forward, starting down the stairs. But I realized too late that I'd taken a wrong step and began falling down a long shaft of air. I knew I would hit the hard edge of the bottom step. I resigned myself to it and relaxed into the fall. I woke up.

The third dream slipped away, forgotten.

Gates of ivory, gates of horn. Dreams, magicians of metaphor. How often, confused and uncertain, we invoke tropes of dislocation. We are disoriented, out of place. When I sat up in bed, I knew these traveling dreams had sprung from my two greatest fears: not knowing and not knowing my way. In the first dream, someone took over my usual role, and I lost my place. I didn't know the rules of the game; I couldn't find my way. I forgot what question I'd asked; I was lost. With an unfamiliar road ahead of me, unsure of the rules or even the questions, what did I know? What would I find? How lost would I be?

I could see that the second dream answered the first. Both women in that second dream seemed to be me. The first wanted to go somewhere but was unsure where; the other me, the driver in control, was afraid to give in to her desires. But the woman who walked through the dark found herself in a familiar place. Falling, she let go of fear. The dream said, be the uncertain traveler. Venturing into uncertainty, I would find what I needed. Letting go, I would be safe.

The last thought I'd had before falling asleep was that cancer is like a foreign country. You enter not knowing the language, customs, or codes. You have no map, and nothing looks familiar. No landmarks to navigate by, no reference points to recall. And now you have to find a way to move through new terrain. I realized as I put my suitcase in the car that morning that cancer had already taught me how to navigate the unknown. The two of us took our seats in the car, cancer riding shotgun and holding on to the maps.

My dreams suffused the car like sunlight. When chilly air began streaming through the car vents, I realized I'd left my coat back in San Francisco. I laughed. Wisely, symbolically, I'd left home unprotected from the weather. Gold-spangled aspen groves lit up the foothills, the half-bare woods filled with sky.

Now I know what people mean when they talk about ghosts. A pressure on the retina, a thing visible but unseen, a firing of synapses so persistent it gives absence density and form. My parents came along for the ride. They sat in the backseat, smiling and relaxed, eager to see the mountains. An image from a family photograph, both of them in their thirties, handsome and well dressed. My dad in his snappy red cardigan, my mother with frosted hair and polished nails.

This may give the wrong impression. My mother was as modest as my father was vain, as self-effacing as he was self-involved. There was nothing hard or brittle about her, none of the hauteur you might associate with frosted hair and manicured nails. She was, in a word, sweet. She wasn't a natural beauty—her nose was too long, her jaw too small—but she was polished, put together, perfumed. Her sprays and spritzers hailed from the ballrooms of her girlhood, the world I glimpsed as a child when she fox-trotted across the living room, dipping and twirling with an imaginary beau, spinning Frank Sinatra on the hi-fi. Even in her hardest years—divorced, depressed, working two jobs, barely hanging on—she never left the house without lipstick and perfect nails. She never taught school in anything but heels. To me they were signs of a spark she protected, nurtured, and carried through the dark. Here in the car, though, those dark times still lay in the future.

An hour outside Denver, the three of us stood atop Lookout Mountain next to Buffalo Bill's grave. In silence and sunlight, we looked out over the distances, the plains sweeping out to the east beyond the curve of the horizon, the Rockies' jagged ranges towering over the west. A view as vast as Bill Cody's ambitions and immense as the myths that grew up around him. Pony Express rider, Indian fighter, buffalo hunter, scout with Custer's Kansas Seventh during the Civil War and the Kansas Fifth after, soldier in the U.S. war against the Plains Indians, Cody lived his life on the stage of westward expansion. And on the blurred edge between life and legend. By 1870 he'd become such a celebrity that in a stage production of *The Scouts of the Prairie*, he played the role of himself. And when it seemed the frontier would close, Cody simply packaged it and took it on the road. In 1883, seven years before the massacre at Wounded Knee would suppress the last Plains Indian uprising of the nineteenth century, Buffalo Bill Cody's Wild West sold tickets to its first show. Throughout the states and Europe, his three-ring spectacle would showcase the dime-novel exploits of the American frontier for the next twenty-six years.

How quickly myths arise and ossify, eliding the complexities and contradictions of what's real. That morning in Denver, crawling along with the morning traffic, I'd heard a radio talk-show host ranting about the Washington sniper, who'd struck again overnight. Spouting something about Al Qaeda, the man opined that foreign terrorists must be loose on American soil. That fear, which had fueled so much anti-Muslim vitriol over the previous months, sat in my mind alongside the legend of Bill Cody. He'd believed in the greatness of a national destiny that had seemed manifest to so many. And yet that destiny had also meant the conquest of other nations' lands, the slaughter of the buffalo, and a thousand Wounded Knees.

Those thoughts kept me out of the Buffalo Bill Museum, with its guns and buckskin fringe. They didn't keep me from feeling moved by the landscape, awed by its scale and the amplitude of the sky.

But moved, too, because those High Plains and high peaks, William Cody's two different worlds, had been the ground of my own myths and complexities, the two geographies of my childhood.

Time and again as they moved, my parents had passed this place between mountains and plains. What were they thinking now, looking west to the Rockies, where my mother had first fallen in love with Aspen? And what did they think looking east toward Kansas, where they'd taken their unhappiness and settled in?

PART ONE

....

Going Back

We long for place; but place itself longs.
Human memory is encoded in air currents
and river sediment. Eskers of ash wait
to be scooped up, lives reconstituted.

ANNE MICHAELS
Fugitive Pieces

....

CHAPTER TWO

The Good Land

I shiver in the backseat in the corner against the door. I hold my cheek against the cold metal until it hurts. I hold myself very still. I am five, and we are moving away. My father drives. My mother sits next to him and says nothing. I will not look at them. Instead, I stare out the window and hear the car tires slub, slub, slub on the red brick streets. My chest hurts. The narrow dark windows of my school slide by—window, window, window, window. I can't see in. But I know that Mrs. Little's kindergarten is going on without me. The children are using quiet voices, cutting paper and coloring, reading and writing in the big yellow workbooks with smooth, dry pages and an elephant on the front. They are listening to stories and taking a quiet nap on cool mats with the lights turned out. I had waited a whole year for school, while my older sister fell in love with Mrs. Little and sat in a circle on the braided rug and came home singing new songs. All of that has been mine for less than half a year. I can hardly breathe. My throat aches. I do not speak or cry. We turn a corner and the brick streets end. We are moving away.

Goodland, Kansas, was not the first place we left, but it is the first I remember leaving. It is my earliest memory of any kind; but no, that's not quite it. I remember losing my first tooth at the Dairy Queen and going to the Halloween party at the one-room school where my mother taught just down the road. But this memory of leaving comes back glistening and whole, an image in amber. A single moment trapped in the sap of a seeping wound until it has hardened in place, unchanging and burnished like a jewel.

Forty years later I was headed back.

The day before, in Pueblo, Colorado, I'd sat in the car in a parking lot, feeling worn out and confused. I'd spent days tracking down the first seven of my thirteen addresses in four different Colorado towns. I'd been to two houses in Grand Junction, two in Montrose, one in Colorado Springs, and two in Pueblo. By the end, the houses had all begun to look the same, all clapboard ranches in what had nearly always been new suburbs. Their numbing sameness seemed the only story I could put together, my parents riding the midcentury wave of upward American mobility. That story I could understand. But the profusion of houses puzzled me. Why so many in so few years? When did we live where? I tried to pencil out a timeline. I knew I'd been born in Montrose, and then we'd moved to Grand Junction. But when? And left Grand Junction when?

I pulled out my mother's address list and, for the first time, really studied the few moving dates she had written down. They were all from our Colorado years, as if to say, "pay close attention here." Between my birth and age three, we'd moved three times. Then my sister Shannon was born. When she was three months old, we left Grand Junction for Colorado Springs, where we stayed for two months. Whoa. Moving with a three-month-old, staying for two months, then packing up again, this time for Pueblo? There we spent seven months in each of two houses and then decamped for Kansas. Altogether, that meant seven moves in four years, the last three moves in the space of eight months, the last four in eighteen.

I felt stunned. I didn't know what to feel. Of course I'd known about the thirteen addresses. But what had it been like, not just to live in so many places, but to move so often, to hear, just after the last box had been unpacked, or not even, that another job had failed, that another, better chance lay just over the next hill. My mother must have done nothing but pack, unpack, change diapers, tend children, house hunt, clean, launder, and feel what? Worry? Resentment? Anger? Fear?

An edge of unease pervaded the childhood I do remember, as though the dread and anxiety of those Colorado years had trailed us into Kansas. By the time my moment of leaving Goodland became enshrined in its golden ark of loss, I'd already lived through uprootings that, while unremembered, have seeped into my bones. Even now whenever I move, their ghosts rise like a vapor. I may be moving for a great new job or into nicer digs, but on my first evening in the new place, I know I'll end up sitting on the floor amid the boxes, sobbing.

No wonder Kansas had never felt like home. The place wasn't ours by birthright or desire or attachment to the soil, but by accident. The same reckless wind that had blown us about the Rockies hurled us across the High Plains into Goodland and would fling us farther east into Hays. Until finally, its energy spent, it dumped us hard in Wichita. A feeling suffused my childhood that my parents, my two sisters, and I belonged elsewhere, that we had never meant to come. That we might not be here long. In Kansas we were out of place. Unrooted and uneasy.

This hardly makes us unique. Frontier chasers, alert to the main chance, Americans move. Everywhere, I meet people like me, some with more addresses than mine. When she lived with her parents, one of my students had moved every six months since she was born. Now every six months, she feels compelled to rearrange her dorm room and repaint the walls. Like me, she has learned not to get too attached. We migrants aren't "placed persons," in Wallace Stegner's terms, "lovers of known earth, known weather, and known neighbors both human and nonhuman." Instead, we "drag [our] exposed roots and have trouble putting them down in new places."

Stegner didn't seem to mind his tumbleweed childhood too much, blown from one frontier to another—Salt Lake, Saskatchewan—by a father who was a dreamer like mine. But once the frontiers have all been mapped, American restlessness can turn inward until it becomes an anxiety of spirit. It did in our family. We knew nothing about place but the drive to stay aloof or to keep on moving through. As the family myth developed over time: it was all my father's fault.

He grew up in California—San Francisco, Sacramento, but mostly L.A.—the third and youngest son. During his toddlerhood, the Dust Bowl years were on, and Midwest farmers, desperate and starving, were streaming toward the orange groves out west. Ralph Seeley already lived at the end of the rainbow, that great place of contradictions where America sent its dreams and dysfunctions. His own parents had migrated from Detroit, and their on-and-off marriage bred its own atmosphere of insecurity. During the off-again times, he lived with his mother, while his older brothers stayed with their father. He didn't even know he had brothers until he was three or four. Both households seem to have moved like nomads. My uncle Carl reports seventeen addresses in L.A. alone before he finished high school.

California during my father's childhood had been no more settled than his family. In his grade school years, the state was rent by conflict between workers' unions and their state-sanctioned, violent suppression; between migrants and anti-immigrant crusaders, the "Okies" only the most recently reviled; between minority hopes and a Jim Crow culture; between the dream and obstacles to the dream. The year he turned eleven, *The Grapes of Wrath*, *The Big Sleep*, and *The Day of the Locust* all showed the land of promise in thrall to big money, big muscle, and big lies.

War marked my father's adolescence. I can only imagine him as a twelve-year-old the winter Pearl Harbor galvanized the West Coast, or guess how he felt, or even what he knew, as California unleashed its good and evil energies. Douglas, Lockheed, and the California shipyards started churning out planes and ships; troops mobilized; and the state became the staging ground for action in the Pacific Rim. Anti-Japanese sentiment, long simmering in California, turned fearful and virulent. New laws labeled Japanese-born citizens and their descendants dangerous aliens, stripped them of their businesses and homes, and shipped them off to internment camps for the duration of the war.

Surely my father felt the exhilarated purpose of Californians preparing for war, his neighbors pouring into shipyards and factories, boys and brothers turning soldier. But what did he feel watching Japanese American neighbors being taken away in trucks and trains? Outrage? Relief? Did he even think much about it?

I knew him so little. I imagine his Los Angeles streets filling with soldiers and sailors on leave between boot camp and battle, the city alive with the high spirits of young, fit, amped-up men. I envision him, a teenager, bounding up the front steps of Hollywood High, just down the street from the Hollywood Canteen. Three million troops would pass through the Canteen by war's end, drinking, eating, and dancing with the likes of Rita Hayworth and Hedy Lamarr. My father would have seen the soldiers milling outside, heard the music spilling into the street. But he would have been too young to join in.

What must it have been like to stand on the sidelines looking on? To be fifteen in 1943 when so many young men, only slightly older, had joined the action? To be fifteen when carloads of newly crew-cut, uniformed soldiers drove through the city looking for prey—the slick, duck-tailed Mexican American teenagers in zoot suits whom they taunted, harassed, and brutalized? The so-called Zoot Suit Riots had to have fascinated, even riled, an adolescent boy. But did my father root for the soldiers or the zoot-suited teens?

This memory comes to me: We are driving somewhere in California; it is dark and we're on vacation; I am eight; my father's mother, Vivian, is in the car. Suddenly, out of the dark, frighteningly, because it makes us swerve and slam on the brakes, a man darts from the other side of the road and flags us down. We roll to a stop; and my father, angry, cranks the window open and asks what the man wants. My grandmother's fear fills the car. The man gestures to his own car across the road as though to explain. He might have a flat tire or run out of gas. Whatever he needs, we do not give it, and then we go on in the night. My grandmother swears, says "stupid Mexicans."

I never heard my father say anything like this. But would a white L.A. teenager have sided with Mexicans? His older brothers were already soldiers, so he would have felt that loyalty and that desire. And if he believed the papers, which fanned rumors of zoot-suiter violence, he might even have cheered for the soldiers who beat up and cut the hair of the boys in fancy dress. But if he could have kept his racial distance, wouldn't that flamboyant, outsider style still have riveted a boy already drawn to theatrics and his own rebellions?

Of course, he couldn't join them. Instead, he dropped out of school and, at seventeen, joined the U.S. Merchant Marine by lying about his age. A year later, in 1945, he quit and enlisted in the Army. He got as far as Italy, but by then, he'd missed the war. Eventually, he found his way to radio and later, TV. His having been born the same year as TV and the talkies made it seem a perfect fit.

While I was growing up, he produced programming and sold ads; but mostly he was "talent," recording voice-overs or selling RCA TVs on TV. And during one short period, when for once we had money for nice clothes and family vacations and a Vista Cruiser station wagon, he anchored the Wichita evening news.

During his years on the news desk, we settled into our thirteenth house, on Magnolia Street in Wichita, and into a feeling of having arrived. It allowed my parents to look back at Colorado with something like nostalgia and to speak its names as though of a time that had been good and sweet. Maybe that's why we rented a cabin in Estes Park for a week the summer I was eleven.

I remember that trip as tranquil and easy, my parents content and happy. The drive from Kansas to the mountains felt free of the tension that often lurked beneath their talk, like snags below the waterline. Instead, the days felt light, unburdened. Perhaps the reason lay in events from the week before.

Days before we were to leave, my mother wrecked the Vista Cruiser. I was in the backseat, barefoot and unbuckled, still dripping and shivering from an hour in the neighborhood pool. Blocks from home, my mother eased into an intersection—someone said she rolled through the stop sign—and as time slowed and slackened, I watched the beat-up Chevy pickup closing in, saw the alarm in the young driver's eyes, the unblinking stares of the two small boys who stood on the truck's front seat holding ice cream cones. I felt the jolt, felt the thud of my skull against the side window, heard metal crunch and glass shatter, watched my mother's head snap forward, heard her cry out, and saw the two little boys fall onto their bottoms on the truck's front seat, still hanging on to their ice creams.

In the stillness that followed—before people came out of their houses to help and to stare, before the other driver climbed out of his cab to see if anyone was hurt, before the police were called and came, before a woman brought a towel and sat with us on the curb, before my father arrived and drove us to the emergency room—my mother turned to check on me. Blood was streaming down her face.

We left for Estes Park anyway. My mother had eight stitches above her eyebrow, an impressive shiner, and a new pair of sunglasses. Yearning for attention, I'd hoped for a little broken bone or even a concussion. But, not even a scratch. A certain tenderness entered the house; and when the Vista Cruiser couldn't be repaired in time, nobody complained. The five of us pared down our luggage and crammed into my father's green Beetle.

I loved the bug. A ride through the city with my father always felt like Mr. Toad's wild ride—me gripping the underside of the seat while he went careening, squealing around corners, clutching, shifting, whistling "Jimmy Crack Corn," and snapping his fingers to change the red lights to green. The Beetle was built for thrills. But not for the long haul. Gone were our languorous family drives, the three of us sprawled over the backseats of the station wagon fighting over the way-back, or with the seats folded down, lounging in our pajamas on the long, flat bed. No more cloud gazing through Vista Cruiser windows. Wedged in the backseat of the Beetle, we three children could barely move. I complained of exceptional misery. Surely no one suffered like me, a tall, long-legged child with no room for my elbows or knees.

Our first night found us cranky and aching in Denver, without hotel reservations during convention week. We took what was left, one room in a no-star motel with not enough beds and a single anemic fluorescent light. My whining won me the prize of a real bed instead of a roll-away; and while I waited for the pain in my knees and hips to soften and slide away, I watched a gaggle of flies gathering on the ceiling.

The mountains erased the journey. I remember bare feet in mountain grass as cool and soft as moss and studded with clover, and the name of the man who owned our cabin, Mr. Christmas. I also remember dinner in a restaurant with a white tablecloth and wine. My father swirled the little splash of wine in his glass, inhaled, tasted, and nodded to the waiter. The man poured two glasses, tipped the bottle upright, settled it into the ice, and left. My mother stared at my father, mouth agape.

"How did you know how to do that?"

He beamed. "I read it in a book."

Maybe the whole story of that week's happiness appears in that moment. For the first time in their married life, my parents had money for restaurants with tablecloths and wine. For the first time, my father—now a handsome, televised man, recognized around town—could nod to a waiter, who would, without question, pour the wine. In that moment, that week, that year, my father pulled off a role he had never been groomed for, wearing a gloss he'd worked hard to acquire.

While the years of plenty lasted, my sisters Tara and Shannon and I were fawned over by secretaries at KARD-TV, and even by Major Astro. Every day after school, watching the helmeted Major strap himself into his rocket ship and say, "Hang on, boys and girls," as he blasted off into Popeye cartoons, we knew that he was really my father's friend Tom Leahy, who smoked cigarettes.

I hoarded the treasure of belonging to a glamorous, famous man. The first moments of his homecoming after doing the evening news were especially sweet. Twenty minutes after he said goodnight to Wichita through the glass of our TV screen, his Beetle chirred into the driveway, and we knew that in seconds the door would open and we'd have him to ourselves.

"HELL-OOOO," he'd say, making his entrance, his announcer's voice filling the room. Remembering his deeply resonant baritone makes me think of barley honey—dark, sun-warmed, and smooth. And the voice never changed. Whether recording spots for RCA or playing Dad at home, he sounded like a newsman delivering the news.

But my father's attentions were all too brief, and he was often absent. Dad chafed against fatherhood and hated being introduced by my mother as her "husband"; he had greater roles in mind. Photogenic and charismatic, but unschooled and beset by his own inner weather, a lost boy in the body of a matinee idol, Dad lived according to the myth of his undiscovered cinematic greatness. And just as film noir's golden land seethes with ill-omened desire, his movie dreams were fueled by darker needs. The father he had rarely seen had acted in Hollywood and died when my father was only eighteen. That missing father became the man Dad idolized and emulated, the man whose notice and approval he hungered for throughout his life. That meant making it in the movies and taking to the stage. Or at least that's how I explain it myself.

The only time I ever saw my grandfather Leon Seeley, stage name Leonard Ceeley, was in the Marx Brothers' *A Day at the Races.* Wearing a dark, tailored suit, a white pocket square, and an Errol Flynn moustache, he plays the dapper Whitmore, business manager of the Standish Sanitarium, which is perched on the brink of foreclosure. He also plays foil to Groucho's manic Hackenbush, a horse doctor impersonating a people doctor who's the new head of the sanitarium. In one scene, Groucho and my grandfather appear on a split screen, speaking to each other on the phone. My grandfather, Mr. Whitmore, intent on exposing Groucho's fraud, thinks he's reached the Florida Medical Board. But in the next room, Groucho has intercepted the call and impersonates not only the medical board but the switchboard operator and a hurricane, interrupting the call every five seconds by switching on the intercom and hollering, as Dr. Hackenbush, at the increasingly agitated Whitmore to keep the noise down.

I've watched the film three times; and each time, instead of seeing Mr. Whitmore, I see a grandfather I never knew saying "veddy" and "teddibly" in that stilted accent of the Hollywood thirties and looking like people I know. He has my uncle Bob's and my sister Tara's jawline; my father's dark, wavy hair swept back from a sharp widow's peak; my dark eyes. I pause and rewind, studying the way he holds his cigarette, brings it to his lips. He has my father's way of smoking, my father's wrists and hands.

Leon earned credits in only two other films, *Moonlight Murders* and *The Sign of the Cross*; but that was enough to set my father's course, and ours.

Besides working at KARD-TV, Dad played in summer stock *Carousel* and dark winter dramas like *The Wall*. There was also a sci-fi flick that started with him and his friend Wayne hammering a model spaceship together in the garage and ended on the dead-fish-smelling shores of Lake Afton one sweltering afternoon as tech guys hauled the spacecraft on a guy wire to simulate intergalactic travel. My sisters and I, bored and blistered from the sun, watched the proceedings while mosquito clouds rose from the mud until welts and bloody specks covered our ankles and arms.

He also performed with the Crown Players in god-awful summer melodramas like *The Moonshiner's Daughter, or He Loved Her Still*. Every year, the troupe cranked out another one, with the same stale off-color jokes between acts and the rinky-tink piano telling us whom to root for and whom to boo—marches for the hero, melodies for the maiden, dark arpeggios for the villain. During one show—who can remember which?—my sister Tara and I worked backstage. I stood on a ladder in the wings, tossing fistfuls of plastic snowflakes into the face of some Sweet Emily or other. It was meant to look fake and it did, and everybody laughed. As teens, the two of us donned 1890s skirts and ferried setups and popcorn to the liquored-up audience, who booed and cheered and shouted warnings to the heroine. She never saw what any fool could see, and always had to be rescued.

My father usually played the villain. He'd sweep aside his black cape; twirl the pointy ends of a mustache he'd grown for the part; and in a leering aside, reveal his dastardly plans to cheat Sweet Mary and her aged mother out of house and home. It was the role my sisters and I would cast him in from the time we were teens and then for the rest of our lives.

The gravy days of the nightly news lasted only four years. As American success gets counted, it was my father's greatest era, better than anything that came before and everything that came after. When it ended, he was forty-one. Then the whirlwind plucked him up and carried him off. This time, he went alone.

My parents were wanderers long before they married. They met on the far edge of the American frontier, in Juneau before Alaska became a state. My father had landed a radio show; and my mother, Beverly Nelton, had gone to teach kindergarten. It was about as far as she could get from her home in Balsam Lake, Wisconsin. I think that's why she chose it.

For me Balsam Lake meant a house on a hill with an apple orchard and a stream at the bottom of a ravine, soft summer grass, picture windows, and bird feeders. Visiting meant filling the little glass bins for the birds. First we filled a coffee can from a barrel full of sunflower seeds, striped and pungent and plenty; and then from inside the den, we watched the drama unfold: orioles, nuthatches, and blue jays flitting and diving, vying with the acrobatic genius of the squirrels, who could outsmart every contraption devised to keep them from stealing the seeds.

Balsam Lake also meant us walking uptown to the drugstore for hot fudge sundaes and Grandpa walking home from his law office for lunch. He smelled of pipe tobacco and Black Jack gum and called me "Pal." And it meant trips to the Twin Cities with my chic, imperious grandmother, who asked for "Better Dresses" at Dayton's and, later at night in the fancy hotel, passed a box of See's chocolates from her twin bed to mine. We called her Gigi. "G," she said, "for glamour."

My mother's Wisconsin was less idyllic. She adored her adoptive father Earl, a country lawyer who, like Abe Lincoln, had studied law by lamplight, and he adored her. But her mother, Gigi, found her disappointing. I've long thought it was because my mother had the wrong father. But whatever the reason, she never quite measured up. Despite a lifelong insecurity that came of those years, something strong in my mother also survived, including an instinct for freedom. The summer she turned seventeen and changed linens at the Yellowstone Lodge, she set her compass west. Within a few years, she would leave Wisconsin for Aspen, before the boom. There, she skied and taught school and tutored Gary Cooper's child. Next, even farther west, came Juneau. There, where anything might have seemed possible, she fell for the airy nothings that my handsome father charmed her into seeing, a life of happily ever upward, maybe even fame. A story with a real Hollywood ending.

She gave him attention, he gave her his need, they fed each other's hunger until it devoured and famished them both. I suspect that even in Juneau she could surely sense, if not yet see, that my father would repeatedly leave her and one day vanish for good. So used to rejection, she seemed to take it as her due.

Six months after their Juneau wedding, my father ran off with the district attorney's wife. My mother had her chance then. But no doubt drawn in by his regret and need for her forgiveness, her desire for his need, she took him back. They repeated this drama every time he fled to another woman's arms, which, by all reports, was often. And she clung to the wagon against all reason every time it headed for what looked like higher ground.

I know little about my parents' early life together. In my days of crossing and recrossing the Great Divide, their ghosts along for the ride, I felt myself absorbing landscapes they had loved, the scenes reeling out like a celluloid dream—a flash of yellow aspens, a glint of rail lines, and forests, darkly green; the swoop down from Loveland Pass to Glenwood Canyon, where I-70, cantilevered above the chasm, drifted out over open space; the lunar landscape of eroded buttes near Grand Junction; one long view outside Montrose that took in cattle pasture, aspen groves, a pumpkin field, desert, and the distant promise of the San Juan Mountains, their peaks etched with snow; broad open ranch land near Gunnison; and the West Elk Mountains, which cast their reflection into Blue Mesa Reservoir. With every mile, I felt the landscapes they had loved becoming mine, revealing something of who my parents had been.

But there is landscape, and there is the life we live in it. What had their life really been like? When I had visited Montrose, my birthplace, I had little more to go on than a shred of narrative and my own surmise. Both of our houses had been torn down. Only later would I find my father's story, "The Lost Ray," a tale about Montrose that illuminates my parents' marriage.

Five months before he died, he'd sent his stories to his older brother Carl; and when Carl died, his daughter Caren sent them to me. My father's attached letter explains that the stories contain "a grain of truth here and there, like the grain of sand which annoys the oyster into creating a pearl." Then he continues, "I ain't no oyster so the outcome may be less than a shining, literate example. . . . It just proves that a lack of education is no stairway to fame and fortune."

When I first read the letter and heard that voice again, the small boy's prayer for reassurance, I felt impatient and pained. His insecurities made him a beggar always asking for absolution. I wasn't the best father, he would say. I wasn't a good husband. I'm an uneducated writer. They were offered as statements of fact, or of fear, something he hoped others would deny. Not something he planned to change. His letter added that he planned to look for a publisher but guessed he had as much chance of finding one as of winning the Powerball lottery.

I wanted his stories to be good. But they weren't. Promising, I would have told a student, definitely something to work with. Anecdotes with interesting plot points but lots of exposition, the characters not fully formed. It was as though the writer couldn't get out of his characters' way and let them speak for themselves. Nor could he take an examining look at the motives of his narrators, who, my father says, are all he.

Real people, he explains, are hidden behind a thin veil of pseudonyms. My sister Tara had become "Ann"; my mother Beverly Jean, "Jean Anne." I don't appear anywhere but had to laugh at the ubiquitous "Anne," my middle name. Excluded as a character, I still lurk in his stories like a shadow. Just as he lurks in mine.

His story begins in junior high, 1940. My father's friend Ray is depressed. Ray's father hates his "soft qualities"; his sister mocks his dream of becoming a fashion illustrator. He is "twisted in knots" by realizing what his life as a homosexual will mean. One day when he and my father are out riding their bikes beside the railroad tracks, they hear a train coming. Ray dashes onto the tracks, throws his arms open, and waits to receive the oncoming locomotive. When my father realizes Ray isn't kidding, he rushes up the bank and drags his friend to safety.

The story leaps ahead to when the narrator and Jean Anne are living in Montrose with their two young daughters. Ray shows up, broke, homeless, jobless, lost, recovering from a beating in San Francisco. Gay bashers? Rough trade? The narrator wonders but doesn't ask, and Ray doesn't explain.

In Montrose Ray and the narrator read plays together as they had when they were boys. And though the narrator envies Ray's skill and training—Ray can cry on cue—they pass the days more as friends than rivals. But Ray can't find work in Montrose. As the narrator explains, "Western Colorado folks . . . didn't much take to folks with California credentials and a flair for a touch of style in dressing." To fill his time, Ray writes long letters to friends back home.

The rising action: Jean Anne finds one of the letters. Ray has decided it's time for him to take my father away, away from the wife who doesn't deserve him. The letter awakens Jean Anne's terror that the narrator "would one day decide to chase one more sexual adventure and leave her." She gives him an ultimatum—choose. Or "she and the babies were leaving."

The narrator rages, first at the insinuation that he "even needed to choose," then at himself. "She had a right to doubt. I had not always been faithful." Quickly, though, he replaces that anger "with the cold desire to rip Ray's heart from his chest, still beating." He packs Ray's bags and waits with them on the porch. When Ray, returning from a walk downtown, reaches the front walk of the house, the narrator says, "That's far enough." He hands Ray fifty dollars for bus fare and says, "Don't call, don't write, don't come back, ever." When Ray walks away and disappears, the narrator thinks that if he ends up walking in front of another train, too bad.

Back in the house, he and Jean Anne smile at each other and chat about dinner. The story ends, "There may have been more conversation but I don't remember it. I do remember that we slept very close. We were very much in love again that night. A team."

It's all pretty formulaic, very *High Noon* in the showdown scene. But "The Lost Ray" gives me a glimpse of our life in Montrose. My mother would have carried the newborn me across the same porch where the narrator waited for Ray, like the porches I'd seen up and down the block of tiny postwar houses the day I'd made my visit. I'd recently walked the same blocks that Ray had in order to catch his bus, seeing what he saw; and I'd been one of the babies my mother played as her bargaining chip: us or Ray. But more than that, the story takes me inside my parents' marriage. In the narrative we had told ourselves later, my father played the role of betrayer, abandoner, non-payer of child support. The aching phantom limb. All the seeds of that later tale appear in "The Lost Ray"—the man who admits his infidelities, the wife who lives in fear that there will be others. The dance of dread and insecurity, the pas de deux of need.

The first time I read it, the story also triggered a great big "wait a minute." What should I make of my mother's ultimatum, that my father "choose"? Would he really have been tempted to "chase one more sexual adventure," this time with "Ray," his friend Fred Perini? And if there was no choice, as he claims, why does he react so violently to Ray's letter? I'm intrigued by the thought that he might have taken a male lover, or been tempted to. Was his secret life more complex than anyone ever thought? Was he addicted not only to sex with women but simply to being desired—no matter by whom?

In the end, I suspect that my parents' reactions had little to do with Fred or his letter. His words simply gave them a chance to stage a kind of morality play—a melodrama in which my mother could put her foot down without any real fear of my father's leaving her and my father, by spurning a lover who was in fact no threat, could act out atonement for past sins and become my mother's hero.

They were twenty-eight when I was born. But everyone in the story speaks and acts like adolescents, behavior that didn't seem tempered by time. The story's narrator, my father nearing seventy, seems strangely unreflective. No sign that he looked at his early rashness with any kind of wry wisdom. Did he have so little sense of who he was—either then or later?

There were other lovers after Montrose, real ones, each one prompting my mother's humiliation, my father's guilt, his apology, her acceptance, their reunion. Plenty of nights, I would guess, when they "were very much in love again." It exhausted me to think of how many times they rehearsed the same play, how many times we were dragged into it as extras.

Of course, I can't know for sure how the clockwork turned inside their psychic dance. I do know that damage unattended sets figures moving in predictable, unconscious rounds. I know myself. I have limned the steps of my own dance, know which ones they taught me. I've seen, through the therapeutic loupe, how my clockwork turned to end my first marriage. Afraid of being abandoned, I took control of the separation I believed must come, by being the first to leave. Later, I'd been drawn to the charismatic P, a man I sensed would leave me but also believed wouldn't, convinced that this time I could change that story I had learned so well. I believed it right up to the moment he absconded with his Colombian fantasy. I see my parents less clearly than I see myself, but I think I can read the dancers from the dance.

Maybe my mother objected to moving, rather than reluctantly acquiescing to it as I've imagined. In the end, it didn't matter. Whenever the clock chimed a dismal hour, we moved. Even when it dawned on her that marriage was no longer an adventure but a forced march that would embitter and impoverish her, she continued to follow. Years later she explained that, at the time, she'd had only two choices—go home to Gigi or go on with Ralph. She'd chosen the least awful option.

Their trail runs cold here and there, and I don't quite know the order of things. But in the three years after they married, my father's restlessness drove them to half a dozen addresses in California, Colorado, and Iowa. I've only been able to find them for sure in the records of a painfully quick succession of births. In 1955 they buried a baby named Tara in Des Moines, Iowa. Eleven months later, also in Des Moines, my sister, also named Tara, was born. Fourteen months after that, when I came along, they were in Colorado. Three babies, one death, two cities, two states, three years. No wonder my parents had so little to tell, so little they wanted to tell.

Coming back now to Goodland seemed stupidly simple. Look at the map, follow the signs, and drive to the town that I'd mourned for forty years. My parents could have brought us back anytime to visit. But Goodland, like so much else, had vanished into family silence.

Getting there, though, meant crossing the High Plains. They spook me, the plains, where the road rolls on through an open vastness of nothing but yucca and scrub and an unrelenting horizon, where you might drive an hour or more without passing another car, an emptiness that stretches from the mountains toward the east for at least five hundred miles. The High Plains were once the bottom of an inland sea and are now riddled with fossils, an alien and otherworldly place. Hour after hour my eyes kept searching for anything that broke the skyline and the solitude—an upright fence post, a windmill, a cow. A hawk, aloft, circling in a high current, wing feathers rippling.

Empty yet haunted, filled with reminders that our story hadn't been the first to vanish out there. Every few minutes, I passed a gravel driveway that led to a shady spot where a front stoop or front door had vanished. Wherever crops or spirits had failed, the house beneath the trees had dissolved into the landscape, graying as the paint faded and peeled, leaning crazily until the porch gave way, losing its shingles to the wind and its rafters to the rats, its walls buckling as the seasons passed—planting, summer, harvest, snow—falling in, at last, without witnesses or sound. Grass grew in the crevices of stone and rotting wood, absorbing the life of the house into itself.

In one spot, a lone chimney standing in an empty field. A stone foundation, a squat, red brick silo. In another spot, two stone chimneys in the shade of a honey locust tree. Somewhere between Simla and Limón, Colorado, a cluster of three tiny whitewashed houses, each no larger than a nine-foot room, all made of stone. One was a tumbledown pile. One was missing a wall. The third had lost its roof and split open like a melon from cellar to sky. The two halves had fallen in a V, exposing the pale yellow flesh of kitchen walls. Tattered cotton curtains swung from a cattywampus window. The private place of home and tender grace of ruffled curtains, exposed to wind and rain and public view.

I wondered about the people whose ghosts lingered on broken thresholds or sighed through ruined barns. Had they loved and lamented these disappearing places? Or felt defeated and glad to leave them? Places that held the accumulated changes of their lives, their wishes and arguments, longings and disappointments, their work and angers and babies and funerals and potluck suppers and summer storms—all the people who left and the people who stayed, all of them remembered or forgotten or imagined by someone passing by. Wherever someone had lived out a life, I felt a kinship. My own lamented houses, my own abandoned towns lay behind me in Colorado and still ahead in Kansas. I imagined that I knew something of what those people had sorrowed for when it disappeared.

As haunted as the High Plains felt, they also felt familiar, a landscape answering to the one I carried inside me: a relentless land and a scale of time and space vaster than human thought, which, because of its enormity, calls forth mythical imaginings. In America's story and in mine, these landscapes are myth-haunted places, filled with cowboys and Indians and pioneers and the toughness it takes to endure. And the story that, no matter how tough things get, real Kansans stay. They endure. In Goodland the county's collected family stories are even titled *They Came to Stay*.

That story was my story, too, growing up. My childhood brain teemed with pioneers who toughed out drought, Indians, prairie fires, and grasshoppers as they made a world out of nothing. Reading *Little House on the Prairie* under the covers at night, I wondered if I'd ever be able to carry all that water from the creek or go to bed hungry. Or how I would feel getting only an orange for Christmas, if I were lucky.

Compared with people who could raise a barn and sew clothes and grow vegetables and dig a well and slaughter their own cow and make soap and candles with the tallow, we were hopeless. My father appeared on television. Television! And my mother claimed she couldn't sew on a button. Where were the beans from our garden? How would we get through the winter? Where were my homemade clothes? God knows, we never went anywhere to stay. Whenever grasshoppers ate the wheat or Indians burned the barn or my father felt insulted by the weather, we packed up our wagon and moved.

Even so, I'd believed in the Kansas on the state seal—the sun rising over green hills in the east, a steamboat chugging up the Missouri, smoke lofting from a settler's chimney and drifting west, the direction of the future. Two covered wagons pulled by oxen, also pressing west; a farmer plowing a field; two Indians on horseback tearing across the prairie after buffalo, their hair streaming, arrows cocked. Above the scene arc thirty-four stars, for the thirty-fourth state, and the state motto arcs over all—*ad astra per aspera*. To the stars through difficulty.

I'd wanted us to be the winning kind of family, but for me family trauma didn't count. No stars hung over divorce and financial distress; and if we stayed in Kansas after my father left, we stuck it out because we were stuck, not because we were tough. It would take years for me to appreciate our toughness, my mother's strength. At the time, we didn't fit the story. We'd even come from the wrong direction, deserting mountains for plains, Manifest Destiny backward.

Years later, as a graduate student in Austin, glad to be living in books, not in Kansas, I needed something, I said, to do with my hands. I took a sewing class and made my daughters' clothes, threading elastic through baby-sized leg holes, appliquéing flower-print balloons on blue coveralls, and crimping on rivets and snaps. When I needed a break from Reynolds's *Discourses on Art* or Blake's commentary on Reynolds—or my commentary on Blake's commentary—I plunged my knuckles into sticky dough, kneading and pounding until the glop became a glossy cushion and rose, warm and yeasty, in a buttered crockery bowl. Or tended my kitchen garden on the weedy, buggy banks of the Colorado River. One steaming afternoon—the only kind an Austin summer knows—I chopped off the head of a tiny rattlesnake coiled in the shade of the green beans. At summer's end, instead of reading *To the Lighthouse*, I canned peppers and beans, pickles and tomatoes—hot vats of glass jars and simmering brine heating the already sweltering afternoons. My small daughters and I went to local fields to pick strawberries and then home to stir a bubbling pot of jam. As the jam jars cooled, we'd listen for the soft pock, pock of the lids sealing tight.

At night, too tired to read, I quilted. While other students went to colloquia or out for beer on Fridays, I gossiped with my quilting bee, our ten needles pricking the patterns of Indian Puzzle or Drunkard's Path. Phyllis, large and loud, complained about her kitchen, which her husband refused to let her remodel. Having lived there since he was born, he couldn't bear to lose his mother's twenties icebox or decor. Evelyn, nearing eighty and hunched over like a question mark, spoke of her dead husband, an architect, while Dolores, eighty-three, recounted her travels to Japan and her upcoming plans for Egypt. Edna's husband was blind and had retired from the post office. She gave me her recipe for cornbread—no flour, only meal, and buttermilk. I loved their old-fashioned names, these peers of my grandmother Gigi but who didn't need Better Dresses from Dayton's, because they could make their own. They grandmothered me, giving me household tips and hugging my little girls. When I wanted to make a quilt for Kate, my four-year-old, they appliquéd Sunbonnet Sue squares, calico girls wearing floppy hats and button shoes.

Long after Austin, when Kansas crept up through the cracks of my San Francisco life, I realized that all that time I'd spent baking, gardening, sewing, and canning, I'd been working hard at becoming a Kansan, refusing to inherit my parents' unfitness for prairie life.

Eastern Colorado and western Kansas share the same geography, the long, dry, fossil-ridden sweep of the High Plains. The state line is a political fiction. Still, just miles from Goodland, when I passed the Welcome to Kansas sign, something welled up from a deep reservoir I hadn't known was there. Partly giddy, partly relieved,

I felt safe and close to tears. The words came unbidden. I blurted out, "I'm home."

Coming into Kansas, I carried Colorado potshards in my pocket—old photographs, maps, neighborhoods, a timeline of our moves. To envision my childhood there, I have studied old snapshots: me at three in Pueblo, sitting atop our black, lacquered coffee table, my doll Debbie in my arms. Debbie looks off to one side, while I look solemn and bored. Her hair is darker than mine. We're both wearing red. These days, Debbie sits with stiff knees and red lips in a trunk in a friend's garage. Mangy tufts dot her skull where Shannon hacked off her hair one Saturday morning. The inscrutable blue message I wrote on Debbie's forehead never did come off.

And I have the photo of Tara and me at Santa's North Pole, still in business today outside of Pueblo. In a black-and-white photo, wearing black-and-white saddle shoes and matching velvet pants, we sit on the lap of a Santa who looks about twenty, with a hairy shin peeking out above his boot. I'm grinning and leaning against Santa's beard, looking impishly up to something. Tara looks wary and ready to bolt, her body stiff, her right foot kicking my ankle. Some sibling drama, maybe. I can only guess at the story beyond the frame—my grandmother sending velvet pants my parents couldn't afford, someone deciding amid the chaos that at least we should visit Santa. The new baby absent from the photo, maybe home with my mother, who would have welcomed a few hours' respite.

And the one of me in ponytails on a front porch with a latticed wooden railing. When I'd visited that house again in Pueblo, it still had the same front porch, the same rail.

Or the photo of my father reading a Little Golden Book to me and Tara, two blond, unsmiling girls. Dad looks like he knows how handsome he is, his cocked head smiling. Tara and I look blank, our eyes big and sad.

In Colorado I'd seen the houses that had held that sometimes sad and sulky child who wrote secret messages on her doll and later angrily cut holes in her pajamas with the scissors. I'd walked the Main Streets that my parents had walked, revisited their landscapes, admired their views. In Montrose I'd remembered the beginning of the story my mother told of my birth—"We were living in Montrose"—without remembering the rest. I had the images in front of me—the pictures of then, the visits of now. But what had that child been thinking? What had she been trying to say when she wrote on Debbie's face? What went on inside that house with the porch? Was it there where I sat cross-legged for another photo, again on the coffee table, this time in my pajamas, holding yet another new doll, this one with red hair and freckles? Tilting my head back against the wall, I glower; at four, I'd mastered sullen. Below the table sits an unpacked cardboard box. But what was the rest of the story?

Nearing Goodland it mattered that I'd seen those small towns, small houses, vistas. But in the end, I'd collected atmosphere more than facts, a pattern of neighborhoods, a patched-together story of leavings, always leavings. Now, I thought, things would be different. In Kansas I would recognize the ruins and remains. I'd be a native informant.

Of course, in Goodland, my expertise had its limits. Besides that day of losing my school, I remembered a wooden porch that echoed when I tap-danced on it, a heating vent that melted the tasseled tips of my shoelaces, a tree-filled park across the street that I feared getting lost in, a Chocolate Dipped Cone at the Dairy Queen. It wasn't much. But when I saw Goodland from the interstate, hunkered down a mile away under a canopy of trees, my heart leaned toward the exit and I pressed the accelerator down.

Five minutes later, off the highway, I slowed into the outskirts of a small country town, slowed even further past a farm implements dealer and a cluster of grain elevators. No one was around. The rail lines that ran beside the elevators were empty—the only sign of a rail car having been there was a grease stain in the gravel.

So this was the place my parents had left Colorado for? This tiny place on the boundary between nowhere and a thousand miles of wheat? Having spent the past five days in the Rockies, I thought I knew how a heart filled with mountains would feel, how Goodland must have seemed a stunning rebuke of the places my mother had loved—Yellowstone, Aspen, Juneau—all of them lost once my handsome, charismatic father shook off the fairy dust of first romance and became who he was. I sensed my mother's despair. I thought, "Her heart must have sunk." Her phrase.

But what did I know? Maybe the only sinking heart was mine. Maybe she'd been glad to leave Colorado, where two new babies and seven moves in four years had soured her even on mountains. Maybe she believed that in a place so different, things would have to change. And she'd grown up in a town ten times smaller, so maybe Goodland's size—five thousand—hadn't mattered. Like so many rural towns, Goodland was hurting now; but things would have been livelier when we'd lived there, with a sugar beet plant in addition to wheat.

I'd also come into town along the ragged outskirts—never the best view of any town. When I turned a corner at Cherry Street, I laughed with love and pleasure. There on an easel forty-feet high stood a giant reproduction of Van Gogh's *Sunflowers*. We may be small, it said, but look, we have a giant Van Gogh. And if the Kansas state flower was good enough for Van Gogh, it's good enough for us. Let us build a monument to the sunflower. In San Francisco a forty-foot Van Gogh would be just another perfume ad or a pointed statement about art in the age of the bottom line. Here it was a landmark. A destination.

Just past the Van Gogh, Cherry jogged left at the High Plains Museum, Home of America's First Helicopter, and emptied into residential shade. This looked like a town I could love. Sweet pastel houses with wooden shutters, front porches, and miniature lawns. A pale moon bigger than a barn hung heavy and full above a little house, a chalk circle against a wash of blue.

I drove along Caldwell to the grain elevators at the north end of town, then back south down Main. Blue banners hung from every light pole proclaiming, "Kansas: The Good Life." Turned right at Thirteenth, toward Center and my house. A red brick church, Episcopal, on the corner. Chambers Park on my right. That must be the park I remembered. Okay, here. Church . . . empty lot . . . house address 1315. Back up. House 1315 . . . empty lot . . . church. I like the look of 1315, a white house with a screened front porch. I squint, trying to turn 1315 into 1307. No luck. In the empty lot, two narrow cement tracks led to grass and shade and nothing more.

I sat for a long while, looking at the nothing more. I felt blank. Now what?

The week before, I'd gone looking for our first house in Grand Junction, the house I'd been a toddler in, but I was afraid it wouldn't be there. A letter I'd sent to "Resident" at 1115 Mesa, asking if I could stop by for a visit, had come back stamped "NSA." No Such Address. Hoping that someone—my mother maybe or the post office—had simply gotten it wrong, I drove up the 900 block of Mesa, a shaded street lined on one side with the smallest postwar houses I'd ever seen. Then up the 1000 block, the 1100s. On the even-numbered side stood a playing field; and on the other side, where our house should have been, no house. No houses at all, only the buildings of the Mesa State College campus and a two-story student apartment house. In the parking lot, a young woman in shorts hopped off the hood of her car, walked down the drive toward me, and smiled.

I turned away and stared across the ball field toward the low, pale wall on the horizon, the same mesa my parents would have seen from their front porch. But there was no front porch. No such address, no such house.

I did recover something of it later when, back in San Francisco, I popped in a DVD that Shannon had sent of my parents' old home movies. Three children in swimsuits chase each other through a sprinkler, grinning at the camera each time they circle back around.

One of them is Tara, age two and a half. I don't know the other two, an older boy and girl. Then I come into the scene, a fifteen-month-old in a baggy diaper, my skinny chest jutting out as I try to keep up with the other kids. Again and again, I hold my plastic bucket over the sprinkler, trying to fill it, but the water shoots straight up, hitting the bottom of the bucket. Undaunted, I dump the empty bucket on my head and laugh, then start again.

Watching the reel, I caught a glimpse of something in the background, a long, pale ridge against the horizon. The view I'd seen from my parents' vanished front yard. The camera turns and there is the house—pale yellow with white trim, a small cement porch, and new grass. An olive green band runs around the bottom two rows of siding, and daisies bloom next to the driveway. My mother opens the screen door, smiles, waves, and goes inside. Slanted numbers next to the door frame count out 1115. There we are, my sister and mother and I on Mesa Street on a summer afternoon.

In returning the missing house to me, these images made me feel tenderly toward that funny, optimistic child with the bucket, toward the hopes of a young family in a new house. They also helped me know it hadn't all been chaos; there were moments of normalcy and play. Like my Colorado snapshots, though, these were a gathering of pieces, recollection in the absence of memory. But I remembered the house in Goodland, and that recollection now felt unhinged in the absence of its object. If I could have heard the echo under the wooden porch, would I have had my Proustian moment? Would a metal heating grate have melted like a crumb of madeleine on my tongue? With nothing to touch, see, or smell, how could I recover the world of my five-year-old self?

I figured I'd have to look for my madeleine in Chambers Park.

I climbed out of the car, feeling suddenly conspicuous. Why was everything so quiet? In Pueblo, just days before, I'd stood in a cul-de-sac looking at one of our houses and heard the flicker and snap of venetian blinds behind me. I wondered who might be watching me now. The grain elevators peered over the trees.

Starting down the sidewalk, which sliced the park into halves, I switched on like a Geiger counter, ready to detect the radioactive traces of my past. But the scale and shape of the world had changed. The fifty-yard distance across the park would have been awfully hard to get lost in. The iron hippopotamus on its heavy spring didn't register. I stared at the swings. Had there been swings? A white fountain in the center, dry and unadorned, raised not one flicker of a pulse. Surely I would remember a fountain. The shade and the bark of the trees felt familiar, but the feeling said "parkness," not this park. When I picked up a handful of dry, leathery pods that rattled with seeds and smelled like fall, I knew them—honey locust—but didn't remember. Touching them conjured nothing.

No madeleines here. I should have recognized the Catholic church on the other side of the park but didn't. I did remember the Sunday I bounced on the kneeler, spun in the pew, turned the tissuey pages of the hymnal and studied its round black spots, balanced on one foot and then the other, while my mother knelt and stood, said "*etcumspiri-tutu-o,*" and sang when the organ played. I scolded myself throughout the mass to sit still. But I couldn't obey. After church, when my mother told my father I'd been very good, I felt ashamed and sorry—sorry for my mother, who lied to protect me, and for myself, who could not be good for a mother willing to lie.

But that story didn't attach itself to this church. I felt suspended above place, nowhere, a stranger whose memories had no place to settle.

I decided it was all kind of silly, this hope to recover . . . well . . . what? My Goodland, after all, was never this grid of shady streets, but a wooden porch, a heating vent, a narrow row of school windows. My park was not this neat square with a sidewalk and fountain, but unmapped cool shade and a five-year-old's sense of proprietorship and fear. I breathed in my disappointment, and then I let it go. Once I stopped trying so hard to remember, a few memories came, undramatically, like slow bubbles rising from some deep place.

One morning, I was in the park. My mother would have told me to stay close to home, and I remember wrapping my arms around a tree while I watched a teacher with her group of Tiny Tots. When she invited me to play with them, I wouldn't. I had to concentrate on not going too far. Besides, I felt both strange and proud, a girl who belonged to the park and not a visitor like them.

Another story: my sister has fallen from the swings, and I run home for my mother. So the swings in the park were those swings. Or did she fall off a teeter totter? Or was it I who fell, while she ran home for our mother? Or did I jump off, dumping her in the mud? That seems more like it, since I was the reckless one. Once, I found a package of Kool-Aid powder in a park, and Tara, always the elder sister, told me that bad people poisoned Kool-Aid to kill dogs. I promptly licked up the powder, and lived. Had that happened in this park?

That was it. Two or three fragments. My wooden porch and the heating vent still floated unmoored in dream space. My parents, too, had faded, withdrawn from the world. Now that I was in Kansas, I was on my own.

Driving back to my hotel, I didn't remember Main Street either, though I liked its wideness and the red brick paving rubbed smooth by nearly a hundred years of wear. No one went into or came out of United Brokerage or the People's State Bank. No one waited in line for the early show at the Sherman Theater. No one shook hands on the steps of the Loyal Order of Moose. The lights placidly turned from red to green, but I was the only traffic. Headed for the edge of town, I let go of wanting to find more in Goodland than an afternoon in a park I once knew and a handful of memories. I'd take a hot bath at the hotel and settle in with the TV remote.

Then there they were. Two narrow rows of little windows running the length of a low, cream-colored building—window, window, window, window.

Our bodies remember as well as our minds. I felt electric, a current skittering up my spine. A five-year-old's grief welled up in my throat. My school. I had carried it so long as a place so irretrievably lost, I hadn't even thought to look for it. But here it stood in the world of concrete objects, with KINDERGARTEN spelled out in big block letters over the central doors. Children's drawings were taped to the windows.

When Odysseus returns to Ithaca after twenty years at war and at sea, in lands of danger and seductive allure, always hungry for home, he comes at last to the house he built with his own hands. Homer describes how Odysseus, disguised as a beggar, came

> through his own doorway . . .
> humped like a bundle of rags over his stick.
> He settled on the inner ash wood sill,
> leaning against the door jamb—cypress timber
> the skilled carpenter planed years ago
> and set up with a plumbline.

Sitting against the sill, he remembers, fitting memory and body to the physical place, the place he made and that made him. In that tender moment of his hero's return, Homer knows the power of place to survive exile and to be reconstructed through a touch.

Through all my life's wanderings, my kindergarten had waited unchanged, not knowing that I carried it with me, an unsolved, inconsolable longing. Standing in front, red brick streets underfoot, I leaned my heart against the doorjamb and felt the cypress timbers, the solidity of place giving solidity to me.

I know how it shaped me, how those afternoons on the braided rug confirmed me as a lover of books, how all the books of my life have been versions of the yellow one with smooth white pages and an elephant on the cover. And I know how losing this place changed me, a child who turned inward and carried her grief like a shield against loss. In that moment of leaving, I became my parents' child, carrying exile with me as a state of being, unattached to any place.

....

CHAPTER THREE

Amazing Grace

That night in Goodland, I thought I wanted to eat local food, sink into local culture. So I asked the dark-haired boy at the hotel desk to recommend a place for dinner. No Pizza Hut or Dairy Queen, something down-home. "Sure," he said, standing up straighter and slapping a xeroxed map on the counter, "there's lots of good places." With his official Comfort Inn pen, he began to trace the restaurant route as though we were driving in a tiny car. "Now you drive along here," he said, and looked up to make sure I understood. "And then right here," he said, making an X next to the High Plains Museum, "is Crazy R's. That's burgers and stuff. Then around this corner," and he turned the paper on the pivot of the pen, "that's burgers." X. I nodded, uh-huh. I thought, uh-uh. No burgers. We continued driving, and there was the Safari Steak House. Okay, I thought, local means meat—I'll eat meat. The best steak house in the county. Everybody goes there. X. My stomach pinched. What it really wanted was a lovely heap of organic baby greens with a splash of balsamic, maybe a fillet of grilled wild salmon bathed in a ginger lime marinade, a crisp glass of chardonnay. Crème brûlée with a soupçon of lavender.

Clearly, I was a spoiled brat.

Still, I didn't want to be one of those tourists who expects the locals to speak my language or cater to my foreign palate. So politely, offhandedly, I inquired, was there anyplace, you know, I might be able to get a little salad? "Oh, sure, anyplace has salad." I knew the salad he meant. A chunk of no-color iceberg with hard, pink tomato wedges tucked around the edges and Thousand Island coagulating on top. Uh-huh, I said. I smelled doom.

"Then right here [X] on Main Street," he said a little apologetically, "Chinese."

Chinese? I said.

"Yeah, China Garden." My heart leapt up. Hello, Pacific Rim. Pea pods and broccoli, even tofu. Could they make tofu in Kansas?

I wasn't sure if we'd reached the end of our little drive, so without trying to sound too eager, I said, smiling, well, that should give me quite a few choices, and I grabbed the map and headed for the door.

By seven, Goodland's streets had shifted from empty to desolate; the soft prattle of my car's tires on the bricks echoed against the buildings. Every store front on Main Street was dark but one, and that beacon in the wilderness was China Garden. More than one of us had been drawn to the light. I pulled in next to five or six cars parked at angles to the curb and went in to look for my kind.

China Garden was a large box of a room, divided into upper and lower levels by a wood railing, like a prairie fence. The prevailing color was brown. The prevailing attitude was, who is that strange woman standing at the front door? Thirty eyes took me in, and I suddenly felt extremely Not Local, a six-foot-tall woman with exceedingly short hair, an unfamiliar face, and trendy eyeglasses standing alone, waiting to be seated. But High Plains dwellers didn't settle a hard land by overreacting, and their estimating glance was so discreet that when they all turned back to their Kung Pao chicken, the shift was as subtle as the landscape. I wanted to say, Hey, I used to live here; I'm sort of one of you. But mostly I knew I wasn't and wished someone would show me to a table.

On the upper level, two steps up from the main floor, a plump blond mother in her early twenties was wrestling a squirming three-year-old back into his booster chair. The young, muscled father leaned on his forearms and kept his head bent over his plate. Two middle-aged couples at two separate tables looked like matched sets, both men in gimme caps and cowboy boots, western shirts with pearl snaps and jeans, both women in large-print tops over slacks, neatly permed gray hair, large glasses, and sensible shoes. Farm couples in town for Chinese food, eating silently together. I wanted to shout, Hey! You're eating Chinese food in Kansas! I wondered if it had taken some getting used to or if they had loved it right away, excited to have something to eat besides big slabs of beef. I thought they should have seemed a little more wowed, but they just kept calmly impaling their stir-fry with their forks.

A smiling Chinese woman, who had been chatting with customers and refilling water glasses, finally led me to a booth on the main floor. Chatty and warm, speaking in what was clearly her second language, she asked if I was visiting somebody; I told her no, but I used to live here. I asked how she'd ended up in Goodland. Really, how the hell had that happened? "Oh, I came with my husband," she said. "Long time ago. Was bored, you know, it's really boring here. So I said, a restaurant, why not? I gotta do something, people gotta eat." She shrugged. "Your waitress be right with you."

My waitress was right with me, a thirtyish woman with dark blond hair. I asked for stir-fried broccoli with tofu, and she puzzled for a minute. "I don't know if they can do that," she said, "it's not on the menu." I suggested that since this dish over here included broccoli and this other dish, tofu, maybe the cook could toss them into the wok, throw on some sauce, and voilà. She shifted from one foot to the other. She'd have to check. She brought back the owner and explained that I wanted broccoli and tofu, in a tone that suggested I'd asked for squid mittens and she blamed herself for not knowing what squid mittens were. But the owner said, no problem, that's okay, and explained how to write it down for the cook. When I asked for chopsticks, the waitress left me alone for a very long time. I studied the Chinese zodiac on the paper place mat, which had been laid out with a perfectly good knife and fork.

Waiting for my dinner, I read the story of Sitting Bull and the Ghost Dance religion in Ian Frazier's *The Great Plains*. All about how the Ghost Dancers at Standing Rock would gather at Sitting Bull's camp, which he'd set up as far from the agency as possible. There, they performed the dance that its visionary Wovoka had promised would bring about the end of white people and the return of the buffalo.

But wait. What was that on the Muzak? It had been nibbling at the edges of my concentration for a while; and now suddenly, I looked up, alert, like a deer scenting danger on the wind. Violins, plaintive, had just swept into the second verse of "Softly and Tenderly, Jesus Is Calling." Nobody else seemed alarmed. My broccoli arrived to the tune of "The Old Rugged Cross," along with chopsticks, and the "Battle Hymn of the Republic" spurred my first foray into the rice. Hymn after hymn, the tape went round while I chopsticked my way through a happy plate of broccoli and tofu.

Just as I was wondering if I could squeeze in that last saucy piece of greenery, a solo flute filled China Garden with a sweet "Amazing Grace." A woman in the booth behind me began humming along, "How sweet the sound." She hummed all the way to "was blind but now I see," and still nobody looked up but me.

But then, why should they? This music came as naturally around here as wheat fields and thunderstorms, music that went without saying, that bound lives together—the Chinese immigrant, the descendants of Polish and German and English pioneers, the waitress, the farmers and their wives, all part of a common world of faith.

Growing up in this buckle of the Bible Belt, I came to learn that the world was divided into thirds—true believers, Catholics, and the damned. Not everyone distinguished between the latter two. But this lesson came later. Until I was eight or so, religion seemed simple. My mother was Catholic, so we children were, too. At eight I made my first confession, though I felt guilty for having so little to tell. "I lied, I disobeyed my parents, and I fought with my sisters" became my ritual confession, which I made without variation every two weeks for years. Wearing a cousin's white dress and a new veil, I also made my first Communion, processing up the aisle carrying two holy objects. From my non-Catholic grandmother, a rosary of cut-glass beads that came from California in a round, mother-of-pearl box lined with red velvet. And from my parents, a white missal filled with colored pictures of saints on slick, tangy-smelling paper and a snap on the front cover that closed. Tellingly, I remember the sensory pleasures of the accessories better than I do receiving the Body of Christ on my tongue.

At home we never condemned the non-Catholic world, where my father worshipped; while we were at Sunday mass, he read novels. He was also allowed to eat meat on Friday, which I feared would send me to hell. When I walked home from school for lunch one Friday, he fed me Thursday night's leftover meatballs. At two o'clock that afternoon, sprawled on the fifth-grade classroom floor coloring my map of Ohio, replete with pigs and silos and the Ohio River, I realized. It was Friday. I'd eaten meat. The guilty taste of tomato sauce and meatballs lingered on my tongue all afternoon, mingling with the smell of crayons and chalk dust.

That night, I confessed to my mother, who assured me that you had to mean to do something or it wasn't a sin. Armed with this new understanding, I pondered the theological implications of a self-willed memory lapse. Could I wipe all the rules out of my mind? Like with brain waves or something?

The year before the meatball debacle, being Catholic had already started to feel odd to me—my friends were Baptist and Lutheran and Methodist, my father read paperbacks, and his brother Bob was Mormon, which seemed entirely exotic. I knew only one other Mormon, a girl in my fourth-grade class. We kids cleverly called her a Moron. And at the time, we knew one other Catholic family, the Archibald's, who had a boy and girl around my age. Whenever we played in their basement, they set up an altar for conducting mass, right next to where a model train with a real headlamp chugged around an oblong track. Pulling eight little B&O freight cars, it whistled around the curves, passed a depot with a flashing red light, and disappeared behind a forest of stiff, cone-shaped trees before emerging on the other side. The train made mass seem dumb and boring. Especially since the boy always got to play the priest.

So Catholic felt awkward, like an ill-fitting shoe; but it never felt like a disadvantage until we moved to Magnolia Street. That year, I met my grim, gray-haired, gap-toothed witch of a fifth-grade teacher, Mrs. Wallace, who, in addition to dragging us through the multiplication tables, introduced us to the Bible game.

The Bible game worked like a spelling bee. I loved spelling and I loved winning; so the first time we lined up for the Bible game, I thought, goody, I'll win. Mrs. Wallace stood us against the chalkboard and handed out little green books with "Gideon" stamped on the cover in gold. What was a Gideon? What were we supposed to do?

Mrs. Wallace explained the rules, then grinning at us with those crooked teeth, said "Ready?" Unready and unsure, I nodded yes and tensed up, poised for the sprint. My stomach fluttered. She called out something like "Deuteronomy 12:1," and all the other kids started flipping through pages, so I started flipping through pages. I had no idea what I was looking for or where it might be. The first kid to find it shot an arm in the air—ooh, ooh, pick me!—and a grinning Mrs. Wallace invited the winner to step forward and read the verse.

"These are the statutes and judgments, which ye shall observe to do in the land, which the LORD God of thy fathers giveth thee to possess it, all the days that ye live upon the earth."

Excellent job! said the crooked teeth.

I was still mulling over the "statutes and judgments" and "giveth" and "ye" when we started up again with another chapter and verse. Again, a flurry of pages and another triumphant hand. Not mine. As a Catholic kid, I had never read the Bible, had hardly heard it mentioned. I didn't realize that the scripture readings at mass came out of a giant-sized Gideon. My mind raced. Where is the book of

Ruth? Who is Ruth? What is 3:16? It all seemed a mystery, but only to me. Everyone else knew the Gideon's secrets; and in the face of her pupils' collective Bible knowledge, Mrs. Wallace beamed.

Little did I know that four years before I ever met Mrs. Wallace, the Supreme Court had declared such games illegal in public schools. Now I suspect that my teacher's rapture hadn't come from her students' success at all, but had sprung from knowing she was getting away with it—with purposefully, defiantly breaking the law. You want statutes and judgments? she was saying, I'll give you statutes and judgments. I'll give you Deuteronomy 12:1.

If I'd only known, I could have invoked my constitutional protections. But all I knew was that my classmates' expertise suggested a world I had never touched and to which I did not belong.

As the game went on, I figured out that the Old Testament came before the New and that the numbers meant chapters and verses, one a subset of the other. But this rudimentary insight couldn't outpace the Sunday school weekends and Bible-camp summers of my peers. They knew all the books in order as well as they did the days of the week. Even bad kids like Kevin D.—who got into trouble nearly every day, had the beginnings of a soft, black moustache, and was kept back at the end of the year—could shine at the Bible game. I, angel student, was a loser.

I knew that Mrs. Wallace would never beam at me with her crooked grin and ask me to read my verse. But for as long as the game went on—and it felt like forever—I bent over my Gideon, furrowing my brow, turning the pages with purpose and desire, all the while keenly aware of my black-and-white saddle shoes, just a little out of focus, against the dusty oak boards of our portable classroom floor.

Thus began my defection from the Catholics. Without knowing what drove me, I begged my mother to free me from the bonds of Saturday catechism class, convincing her it had nothing to teach me. In a sense, I was right. The volunteer teachers usually just read the book aloud or lit a match with the lights turned out in order to dramatize some doctrinal point or other. Jesus, the light of the world? Faith, a light in the darkness? Most importantly, they could never teach me what I needed to learn, how to fit into Mrs. Wallace's world.

I drifted toward the evangelicals, arriving there gradually and in a confused way, still thinking of myself as Catholic even while happily inhaling the ardent, Protestant air of my high school. It helped that ecstatic forms of Christianity melded naturally with the sixties euphoria of the Jesus freaks. In those years of *Godspell* and *Jesus Christ Superstar*, it was hip to groove with Jesus, a rebel with a protest sign that read Peace and Love. Tara and I slapped a "Maranatha!" bumper sticker across the back of our blue vw Beetle, its bright blue letters proclaiming the coming of the Lord.

Our prep school had not been inspired by *Godspell* or other musical passion plays, but I didn't know enough to distinguish one enthusiastic sect from another. The various dialects that swirled off the tongues of my friends all seemed the same to me, the idiom of insiders and the culturally adept. In their presence, I began to learn the language that would have won me the Bible game.

I did briefly resist, when Bible Emphasis Week my junior year featured a speaker who had memorized hundreds of pages of the Bible and had made it his life's work to memorize the rest. By that time, I knew which books came first and which last, and I had a good sense of what lay between Genesis and the fiery end of all things, when the sheep and goats would go their separate ways and the wonders of the Apocalypse would become clear. So I had a pretty good idea of what the man was up against and was suitably impressed. But when our Religious Studies teacher decided that memorizing the Bible would be good for the rest of us, I preferred not to. His assignment, to memorize one chapter, seemed absurd, one of those pedagogical inspirations that runs aground before getting airborne. I've had a few of those myself since then, so I know.

Even then, I had my own ideas about learning, which, unless it involved "To be or not to be" or "'Twas brillig, and the slithy toves," did not include memorizing huge hunks of text. So I traded in all my accumulated capital—garnered by good grades, good behavior, and extracurricular everything—to sit this one out. I never explained my missing recitation, and my teacher never asked. The C he gave me in Religious Studies that term seemed a small price to pay.

Still, I apparently hadn't given up my ambition to impress Mrs. Wallace. Over the years, the Bible game grew underground like a rhizome, where it crept through the dark, feeding itself on my subterranean need to master things that baffled me and my even deeper need to belong, until one day, it emerged blinking in the hot August sun of a tiny Texas town.

I, who with my scores and grades could have gone to college anywhere, followed a friend to Hardin-Simmons University, a Southern Baptist school in Abilene. I got myself a full-immersion baptism at Pioneer Baptist Church, attended hellfire sermons on Sundays and Bible study on Wednesdays, and learned all the great Protestant hymns. When I'd nothing left to prove, I fled midyear to the University of Dallas, back to the Catholics, whom I would later—after several attempts—abandon for good.

In China Garden in Goodland, I felt like an inside outsider. Someone who knew the words, the world view, the winning tricks—but someone who chose not to play. Someone who knew, but also knew better. I felt smugly advanced in my thinking. Besides, I knew how to use chopsticks. The woman humming "Amazing Grace" had nothing on me.

During my weeks on the road, it came as no surprise that Jesus is still the lingua franca of the plains. The Calvary Satellite Network, which beams the Good Word abroad from Colorado, may outreach, but surely does not surpass in earnestness, the more-old-fashioned medium of Billboards for Jesus. Along highways and on fence posts, from Colorado Springs to Indiana, Jesus shares equal space with Denny's and McDonald's and the World's Largest Prairie Dog Village.

Jesus Saves.

Jesus Completely Saves.

Prevent Dis-Ease. Give Yours to Jesus.

Jesus Is Alive!

Seek Christ Today. Tomorrow Is Unknown.

No God, No Hope. Know God, Know Hope.

In between signs and billboards, the Word rides the prairie airwaves, transmitted from small-town towers like KGCR, Goodland's Greater Christian Radio. My resolve to listen to local radio quickly withered as station after station broadcast sermons on everything from the evils of homosexuality to how to love your neighbor. Even when I picked up a signal for classical music, it turned out to be Christian classical, with sermons sandwiched between symphonies. Somewhere east of Goodland, frazzled by navigating between narrow bands of static and stations for Jesus, I switched the dial to "off" and resigned myself to the sound of the wind.

One afternoon, in the bookshop at Fort Larned—one of several forts established to protect the mail, as the commander's orders put it, "during the excitement among the Indians"—I bought a CD of Lakota music. Buying Native music, I figured, would not only give me something decent to listen to but would also put me on the side of Sitting Bull and his Hunkpapa band of Lakota. I laid my purchase on the counter and looked straight into the eyes of the National Park Service ranger, declaring my loyalty. Take that, pioneer, imperialist, evangelist, Ghost-Dance-smashing, white-people Kansas.

In the car, the Lakota wooden flute sounded hollow and haunted, the music simple and strange. I eased the car out of the gravel parking lot onto the highway and turned up the volume, floating down the road on waves of ancient sound. No more sermons and calls to salvation, but music to suit the landscape, which I tried to imagine open and wild, restored to its rightful state as the hunting grounds of the Arapahoe and Cheyenne. I was feeling pretty self-righteous when, four songs into the CD, the flute player breathed out those first few unmistakable notes. The opening bars of "Amazing Grace."

I hadn't figured it out yet, but that night in China Garden, my chopstick-wielding smugness had met its match. When those small-town, cattle-ranching, wheat-growing Kansans didn't marvel over a Chinese restaurant on the High Plains, they were refusing to be herded into my tidy corrals. Why shouldn't Kansans eat Chinese food just as I did in San Francisco? Just because I thought they were supposed to be provincial carnivores? And why should a Lakota flute player refuse to play the white people's song? Just because, loyal to some purist notion of authenticity, I said so?

In the days ahead, Kansas became a rich, complex place that challenged my assumptions and stereotypes about the state I'd left at seventeen. Of the many people I met, not one was anything but authentically curious, generous, and kind. Recovering my fluency in Kansas things, I talked recipes, quilts, and weather with some people, books and poetry with others. I met populists and democrats, poets and farmers, Lutherans and agnostics, and a lot of people who not only loved where they lived but had chosen it. Some had moved away to cities but came back to where people knew them, had known them their whole lives. Many had traveled to Europe or San Francisco but never wanted to live there. Some had never left home. Every one of them listened to my tales of wandering with openness and sympathy, more tolerant of my otherness than I had been of theirs. They seemed to feel sorry for me, gone so long, and welcomed me home.

Back there in China Garden, I should have been humming, "a wretch like me," right along with the woman in the next booth. Lord knows, I could have used some amazing grace to make me more open-minded and less provincial. Less stuck-up about my passport from Oz.

....

CHAPTER FOUR

The Known World

I remembered Hays in neutral shades, the damp beige of winter grass, the brittle beige of summer. Maybe, I thought, time had simply steeped the past in a sepia wash, draining the world of color. But driving into town, I saw that it was the stone. At first, I passed the usual—grain elevators and trailer parks, Jimbo's Paint and Body. But nearly everything downtown—houses, the post office, City Hall, the George Philip Hardware "Since 1894," and a tiny cabin in the town square—had been built of straw-colored stone. The squat architecture, as flat as the horizon and dwarfed by the sky, seemed to have grown right out of the ground.

The monochromatic palette continued in our old neighborhood. Ash Street, pallid and wide, was lined with stone houses and pastel ones, white, pale yellow, and tan. Our two houses, across-the-street neighbors, had been painted two different shades of beige.

I parked in front of the bigger house, a classic ranch of blond brick and siding atop a gentle rise, with a porch awning held up by wrought-iron pillars. I laughed out loud at the sloping driveway that Tara and I raced down on our tricycles. I don't remember if it happened once or a hundred times, but I do remember shoving off from the top of the hill and, picking up speed, the pedals whipping around, hurtling terrified toward the street, wrenching the handlebars at the last second to keep from flying into traffic, then dragging my trike up the hill to do it all again. A dangerously steep incline, I saw, of maybe three degrees.

The darker beige duplex across the street, with two dark doors, had a perfectly level, gravel driveway. Two clipped shrubs and not much of a yard. A perfunctory slab for a porch. No wrought iron, no awning. I didn't know why we'd moved from the bigger house to the duplex, which had one less bedroom and no garage. Some routine marital disaster, some failed financial scheme? That's the house I turned six in. And where, for part of one summer while recovering from what doctors guessed might be a mild case of Rocky Mountain spotted fever, I sat behind the screen door in my rocking chair, watching other kids play in the yard.

I arrived in late afternoon. A giant elm in back of the duplex threw its late afternoon shadow across the roof and onto the lawn. Even when I was six, that tree had shaded the entire backyard, its trunk a dark pillar too big for the house, and too close. Once in summer on a sultry night, I lay on my bed with the windows open, my naked arms and legs sprawled across the sheets. It was bedtime but not fully dark, the way it happens in summer. Sticky with sweat, I waited for sleep, trying not to move so my restless body would cool. The café-style curtains hung open on their gold-colored rings, and I stared out the window at the tree. It was darker than the darkness outside, and the leaves hung without moving.

All at once, in that way a figure emerges from the ground of an ordinary scene—like a raven from a black branch—the dark shape was not just a tree, but a man. A man looking at me. A hot bolt of fear snapped me out of the drowse of heat and he saw that I saw and he started and his startled eyes told me he was wrong to be there, and I felt ashamed that he could see my panties and my six-year-old breasts. For a few seconds neither of us moved. Then I scrambled off the bed and ran for my mother.

When she sprinted back, she knelt on the bed and peered out. I hung back in the doorway, my heart thumping. By then the man had gone. She slid the curtains closed and, pulling me to her, rubbed my back, saying it would be all right, all right now. She told me to stay in the house while she went outside and waited. If he came back, she would catch him. She slipped out into the dark, into the shadow of the tree. From the doorway, I stared at the curtains, knowing my mother was out there, in danger. The man never came.

The next day, all the neighbors knew about the man, and now they would be watching out for him. No one watched more than I did. Every night, no matter how hot, I lay there with the curtains closed and the sheet pulled up, sleepless and waiting.

I don't know whether my mother was especially brave that night and would have done anything to protect me, even confront a man in the dark, or whether she thought I only thought I saw a man and, more clever than daring, reassured me with a ruse of lying in wait. What never occurred to me then was that whatever her role, hero or pretender, she had played it because my father wasn't home.

I rang the bell next door, where our former neighbor Annie still lived. In the years since we'd left Hays for Wichita and then I'd left for college, marriage, grad school, Dallas, Austin, Middletown, New Haven, and San Francisco, she'd kept watch, stayed put, and grown old. She answered the door and smiled.

"You're Beverly's daughter!" Not Ralph's, just Beverly's.

At eighty-seven, Annie's short, curly hair had turned only partly gray. She was fashionably thin, wearing oversized glasses, slacks, and a flowered blouse, her feet in comfortable shoes. We sat in the living room, each of us on a matching floral love seat. The sounds of a game show drifted in from downstairs, the room she called her nest.

"Your mother always kept in touch," she said. Annie knew all my milestones—graduations, marriage, children, jobs—up until Mom's last Christmas letter, four years before.

This continuity in my mother's life always catches me by surprise. She'd stayed in touch with neighbors and friends and students from every place she'd ever lived. Even the week she died, she sent out cards and letters, punctuating sentences with frowns or smiley faces and slapping colored stickers on the envelopes, a first-grade teacher to the end. Her Rolodex, which came to me when she died, was crammed with addresses from across the map, like an unbroken line of cookie crumbs. My father may have burned his many bridges, but she'd tended her trail all the way back to the start.

Annie said she'd missed hearing the news, so we caught up. Her husband Jerry, whom I'd remembered as a tall, skinny man in khakis and dark horn-rimmed glasses, who laughed a lot and barbecued, had died. Her children, teenagers when I was five, now had grandchildren. I told her about my trip, all the old addresses, my wanting to see where we'd lived, put some pieces of my family story together. Annie looked down, paused, as though deliberating, choosing something to tell me.

"Your sister and you wore the most beautiful dresses I had ever seen," she offered.

I remembered them. Smocked, polished cotton with crinolines and ribbons, my orange plaid dress with its starched white pinafore and appliquéd giraffe—a whole wardrobe of dresses sent by Gigi from Dayton's.

"And every week, your mother would take the hems out of those dresses, wash them, put the hems back up, and iron. She did it so the hemline wouldn't show when she had to lengthen the dresses. You know, on account of you growing. Every week she did that. Ten dresses. By hand."

We shook our heads at such craziness.

"Your mother, I think, must have grown up in a house with a lot of help."

She had. The big house in Balsam Lake. Where Margaret Moose came twice a week to wax floors, scrub toilets, and iron my grandfather's shirts.

Gigi had set up the laundry in the basement with long, clean folding tables, an ironing board with a padded silver cover, a sprinkling bottle for dampening cottons, bottles of starch and detergent, stain removers and bleach, and a deep freezer with a lift-up lid. When she took freshly washed shirts out of the machine, she'd throw them into the freezer, where they'd stay, damp and stiff, until Margaret Moose came to thaw them out with the iron.

There, I guessed, next to the deep freeze, the unstitching and resewing of my mother's girlhood hems had taken place, there, the starching and crisping of crinolines, the pressing of satin ribbons—all by Margaret Moose or the half-dozen other women who came to work at my grandmother's over the years.

In Hays, unwilling or unable to slacken her mother's standards, my mother did all of that work herself. It had to have exhausted her. On the other hand, maybe the waxing, cleaning, dusting, laundering, ironing, starching, and hemming had also helped her keep her finger in the dam, hold back the chaos. Until, as always, something happened. Like whatever had forced us to move into the smaller house in Hays.

Annie looked at me, seeming to size up what I might or might not know about my mother's life. I could tell she wanted to say more. I waited. Something dark clouded her eyes. "Your mother had such a hard time."

I held her gaze and said, unsurprised and unflinching, "I know."

I did know something about the hard time, some small things. One day, my mother gathered us three girls together—Shannon was two or three—and explained that Daddy was going to move away. The news settled over us. What did it mean? She explained that we would see him on Saturdays and that she would pack a little lunch for us to take along. She tried to make it sound like an ordinary excursion, nothing to worry about. But her soft, patient voice told me this was something terrible. When we saw our dad, she said, she would not come with us.

I wondered if there would be graham crackers in the lunches, and peanut butter sandwiches cut corner to corner and wrapped in waxed paper. Thinking of those lunches, I wanted to cry. Tara did cry. When my mother asked, I was the only one who wanted to go for a walk. So she took my hand, and we walked outside but got only as far as Annie's yard next door. My mother and Annie talked in low, quiet voices; and I knew it was because of what was happening to us. I poked at the burnt summer grass with the round rubber toe of my tennis shoe and stared into the gutter, where a thin trickle of sprinkler water from somewhere up the block was inching its way through the pale, powdery dirt.

"She did have a hard time," I said to Annie.

Moving into the duplex might have had something to do with the news of bag lunches and Saturdays with Daddy and the talk on Annie's lawn. I don't know how many days passed before I saw my father again, but one day, there he was. Not outside on the driveway on a Saturday, but in the kitchen. My mother wrapped her arms around him and peered into his face, smiling. She embraced him and he embraced her. What was happening? For days, I waited, but Daddy showed no signs of leaving. My mother seemed entirely happy, smiling whenever he came into a room. Nobody told the three of us anything.

Any grown-up could have guessed that they had decided—after who knows what tears and recriminations—to reconcile and try again. But I kept waiting for the lunches. Then I, who had been made to feel sad and ashamed and chosen for special misery, who had been led to believe there would be Saturdays with sandwiches in paper bags, got mad. Someone had made me feel vulnerable and exposed. Someone had to be blamed. I concluded that my mother was a liar.

Annie and I sat silently, not meeting each other's eyes, perched on the brink of revelation. Should I tell her what I remembered? Should I ask her what she knew? Was that really what I'd come from San Francisco to learn?

"It upset me so much when you moved into that duplex," Annie went on. She shook her head and clucked her tongue. "Seeing your mother have to manage in such a tiny place." She didn't say she felt sorry for my father, which confirmed my guess. The move had something to do with something he'd done. But what? Maybe after the separation—had there been only one?—they'd had to economize.

Maybe he'd changed jobs. Maybe there had been another woman. I suspected that from Annie's tone of voice, from the down-turned corners of her mouth.

I had come all this way. I would never have a better informant. Someone who knew our secrets. A friend my mother had kept for forty years. A confidante. "Ask," she seemed to say. "Ask me what happened."

The door opened, but I couldn't walk through.

It wasn't the first time. In Grand Junction, strolling downtown, I'd seen a radio tower rising above Eighth and Main and felt sure that my father had worked at the station there. But I'd felt too timid to ask. I argued with myself. I'd crossed half the continent to stand in the same places my parents had. But when it came to knowing more about my father, I'd fearfully pushed back.

Of course, keeping him at a distance also kept him present, standing just at the edge of my attention, pressing in. Insisting on a role in every story. When I ducked into a used bookstore down the street from the radio station, he followed me in. The store owner sat hunched over an old folio, peering through thick glasses at yellowed pages. He glanced up and said hello, his pale blue eyes huge behind the lenses. He was in his seventies, I guessed, the same age my parents would have been. I wanted to ask whether he'd always lived in Grand Junction, what it had been like when my parents were young. But imagining him forty years younger, his shoulders unstooped and blue eyes clear, I couldn't ask. What if he had known my parents? And what if my father had had an affair with the man's wife?

It seemed silly, but no sooner had I thought it than it seemed true. Infidelity seemed the one central fact of my father's life, the ur-narrative of every other story. Silly, but I couldn't shake it. Improbable, I thought, but not impossible. What if it were true? Then what would the book dealer and I have had to say?

I mustered only enough nerve to ask for a Grand Junction map.

Now at Annie's, I balked again. I assumed the fact of my father's sexual transgressions. Did I really need the details? Was I protecting him or protecting myself? Was it simple, willful evasion? The family habit of looking the other way? Could I trust my sudden conviction that a daughter really didn't need to know the litany of her father's betrayals and failures? Or was the mystery simply safer than whatever I might learn?

More than anything, I think, I didn't want the dark man to emerge from behind the tree. I knew that man, and he wasn't the father I wanted. And I suspected he wasn't all there was to the father I'd had.

Annie smiled and asked if she could get me a glass of tea. The moment passed, and the door closed. She brought the glasses from the kitchen, set them down on coasters, and went to her nest to turn down the TV. She returned with an envelope and, sitting next to me, pulled out two snapshots. One of my parents with the three of us, my mother in a polka-dot dress, her brown hair frosted blond, we girls decked out in freshly hemmed dresses from Dayton's. Everyone smiling, though none of us look like we mean it. Except for my father, who flashes his Hollywood teeth and smiling eyes. In the second one, Annie and Jerry have joined us. A group shot of neighbors. Black and white. Neutral tones.

Unfurl my map of Hays at the age of six and you will see two hemispheres. In the first, two beige houses face each other across a wide, gray space. Ruffled curtains hang in the windows, and red tulips march single file across the yards. A black tree looms over the little house, and a yellow ball with spiky rays shines over the big one. In front of that second house, a red tricycle sits at the top of a slanted line that tips down to the street. Call this hemisphere "Home."

Call the other one "School." Wilson School appears as a long, beige rectangle with a jungle gym outside and two flags flying from the roof, one for Kansas and one for America.

In that corner of the map stands a caged tiger inside the circus wagon that I made out of newspaper and paint when I had to stay home from school eating applesauce and Jell-O after having my tonsils out. In another corner, my second-grade teacher Mrs. Thornbrough's German shepherd stands on its hind legs, towering over her. One day, when I brought her a rose that my mother had clipped from our yard, Mrs. Thornbrough pinned it to her blouse. I spent the day in distress, knowing it would die without water. Standing at the front of the line for afternoon recess, aching for the rose, which was beginning to droop, I finally pointed and said, as casually as I could, "You know, that's real." She glanced down at the rose and, smiling, said, "I know," as though it gave her joy.

This map is also filled with books, beginning with one about a boy whose name started with a *J*. I had never seen the word before, and I stared at it, stumped. I was sitting next to a teacher's desk, auditioning to skip first grade. I knew that reading would decide everything. But with that big *J* name as the very first word, I couldn't even begin.

"Hmm," I said, as though I only needed a second to think about it. She waited and then quietly helped me.

"Jeremiah," she prompted—or maybe it was Jeremy or Jonathon—and I repeated it, watching as a word with that sound, Jonathon, emerged from the letters on the page. As I put on my story voice and started, the tale of Jeremy or Jonathon and his boat began to sail. I kept reading, fluidly and quietly and not too proudly, not making any mistakes, while the teacher listened. I changed my voice for the speaking parts and paused for emphasis or to signal a change in scene. We were just getting to the good part, which I don't remember, when the teacher stopped me.

"Very good." She smiled. So I jumped from kindergarten to second grade. My official career in books could now begin.

While my map of home is iconic—sun, shadow, tulip, tree—and strangely depopulated, my school hemisphere teems with teachers and stories and children and books. There was still room for confusion—a dying rose that made my teacher glad—but at school things mostly made sense. If I read well, I skipped ahead. Arithmetic problems had correct answers that I could figure out by myself. Words meant what they said and didn't change. Stories happened in surprising but orderly ways. School became a world where, unlike home, even a child could know and understand. It gave me the only sure ground I knew.

My two hemispheres float in a wide, unmapped sea. The four blocks between home and school appear empty of streets, houses, grass, or trees. Across the vast, blank field, a wavering blue line tethers one balloon world to the other. One day, well before the tonsils or the man in the tree or the reading audition or Mrs. Thornbrough's dog, I learned the fear of being lost in the space of that unknown world.

My mother had said goodbye to me at the playground fence. Every day for my first week at the new kindergarten, she'd walked me there and watched as I crossed the playground to line up for the afternoon class. Every day, I'd walked more confidently toward the tidy double lines, girls in one, boys the other. I felt my mother's eyes on me, protecting, making sure.

That day, though, when she kissed me goodbye, she said, "Now do you know the way home?" She pointed back the way we had come. I nodded yes.

"Then today, you can walk home by yourself."

My stomach fluttered, but I believed her. She had to know better than I.

That afternoon, I left school, took two steps toward the street, and had no idea which way was home. A row of cars stood angled at the curb, filling up with children, backing out, and driving away. Two teachers chatted together and waved goodbye to one car and then another. Where was the fence? I don't know that anyone had shown me other landmarks (turn right at the stone house, left at the hydrant), but I knew there should have been a fence. I couldn't figure out, and my mother couldn't have known, that when we were let out at the end of the day, we left not through the back door by the playground, but the front door by the street.

I stood, jittery and tense, brain frozen, paralyzed. Lost in a sea marked "monsters."

I never thought to ask for help, afraid maybe to seem inept in this place where right answers counted for so much. I refused to cry, trying to look like a girl waiting for her mother at the end of the day. To anyone else, I surely looked like any bewildered, panicky five-year-old. And so I was rescued by someone else's mother.

Is someone picking you up?

No.

Do you know your way home?

No.

Do you know your address?

No.

Is your house close by?

I think so.

I climbed into the car of the freckled, red-haired mother. Her child, who was either a boy or girl and who may or may not have been in my class, sat next to me in the backseat. While the woman drove slowly up one street and down another, I concentrated.

Is this your house?

No.

Does this look familiar?

No.

Does this?

All the houses looked nearly alike, but none of them quite like mine. And then I saw it. My anxiety flushed away and I pointed, there's my house. My house, my porch, my driveway, and my mother coming out looking puzzled and surprised. The good mother who had saved me told my bad mother, who had abandoned me, that I hadn't known my way home. "Oh, I'm so sorry, honey," my mother said. She tried to hug me, but I shook myself loose and stomped into the house.

I don't remember whether my mother started walking me to and from school again, whether she arranged for other children to walk with me, or whether I repeated the experiment the next day with better instructions. I do know that I got lost that afternoon because

I hadn't told her I didn't know how to get home. And because when I said I did, she believed me.

Not knowing and not knowing my way. Two sides of the same metaphor. Lost. The two fears that, rooted in the two years we spent in Hays, would one day shape my dreams on the eve of this first journey back to Kansas. Knowing the answers in school gave me mastery, security, and reward. Not knowing my way, not knowing the world, led to fear, anger, disaster. At age five, still raw with the sorrow of leaving Goodland, I had amassed more proof that home stood on shifting sands. In my disgrace, I needed someone to blame. For the first time, I knew that my mother could not be trusted.

How often parents fail. Not out of malice, but out of forgetting. Forgetting how children reason, how they can lack the words or the courage to speak their confusion and need. How much they need to have explained. And how little it takes for parents to be heroes. The next year, when the man came out of the dark and my mother braved the night to catch him, I think she saved us both.

When I left Annie's in late afternoon, the duplex had been swallowed up in shadow. I drove the four blocks to Wilson Elementary, a route that on the street map looked like a shallow, square-cornered U. South half a block to Twenty-seventh, east three blocks to Fort Street, north to Twenty-eighth. I parked next to the fence behind the playground. Easy.

Except for his mysterious reappearance in the kitchen when he was supposed to be moving away, my father stands at the center of only one other story from Hays. One day, I came home from kindergarten with a cut above my elbow. I hadn't had the tomboy crushed out of me yet and often sported scrapes and bruises I hardly noticed and couldn't explain. At the dinner table, my father took one look at my elbow, exclaimed that it was bleeding, and asked what happened. This seemed dramatic, so I twisted my elbow around so I could see. The skinny red slice dotted with bloody beads impressed even me.

Who knows what adults really want? My mother had clearly wanted me to know the way home, so I claimed that I did. My father seemed to want some answer to match his distress, so I shrugged my shoulders and replied that a boy at school had cut me with his knife.

There was a boy at school with a knife, a little pocketknife he had shown me on the playground. It had a mother-of-pearl handle and a thin blade that folded in and out. He was tall like me and had a crew cut; and when we lined up in the boys' and girls' lines, I liked to stand next to him. I was what my sister calls father-hungry, and fell in love early and often. This boy was my first crush. We chased each other on the playground, he pushed me on the swings. And then he showed me his knife. It fit in his open palm like a seashell; and when he opened and closed the blade, it seemed ingenious and beautiful. Somehow I knew that knives belonged to boys and made them strong and worthy of love. He once told the teacher he had carried home a big stone from the nearby cemetery, only to find that he'd brought home a gravestone. The teacher seemed doubtful—how could a small boy carry such a big stone?—but I believed him.

Perhaps, when my father asked what happened to my elbow, I could think of no better tribute than to give this boy the power to hurt me, to make his mark of love and attention on my arm. People who loved each other hurt each other, hurt themselves and their children. This much I had learned. Or perhaps this was the most dramatic story I could think of, and I cast my favorite boy in the lead. Or maybe I had to pin my life's hurt on someone besides my parents. Or maybe like most five-year-olds, like the boy with his gravestone, I simply had a penchant for inventing tall tales.

For the next few minutes, I had my father's attention, and this may explain my lie as well as anything. For once, he was there and riveted on me. He raised his voice and vowed he'd see the principal, demand that the boy be punished. My mother, more savvy perhaps in the ways of the childish mind, quietly asked me, "Honey, are you sure?"

Even though I sensed that my father's ire might be a bit overdone, I could see I had unleashed something huge. But since telling the truth now would only make things worse, I stuck to my story. I did soften it with the addendum, "he didn't mean to."

Angry words and phone calls must have followed, accusations and meetings at the school. But I don't recall them, and as far as I remember, no one asked me for my story again. The denouement unfurled some days later on the playground when I shyly asked the boy if he wanted to play on the swings. I had on my favorite lavender plaid dress with the pleats and the white collar. I wondered if his knife was in his pocket.

"My father told me not to play with you," he answered. I nodded wisely. I deserved it.

I thought of that boy again when I left the neighborhood and passed the cemetery where he'd picked up the stone. Red plastic geraniums and little American flags dotted the manicured grass. What was that boy doing now, a man nearing fifty? Did he ever think of the time he had stood powerless in the face of a lie he could denounce but never disprove?

When I think of the knife and my father and the boy, it all seems of a piece with our life in Hays. It was a season of lies and suspected lies, of confusion and bruised trust. Of figures emerging from the dark to teach me fear. A time when my need for the truth outstripped my parents' willingness to speak it. And my need for attention and rescue overpowered my courage to say what was true.

Off the mainland of my known world floats an archipelago of pleasures: Bike's Burger Bar, where my mom, her friend Jo, Jo's two daughters, and the three of us, all crammed into Jo's '55 Buick—all bulbous hood and fenders and crushed velvet seats—loaded up on burgers and fries, and ate them in the band shell in the park. Or the WPA swimming pool, with its art deco limestone pool house, where, in summer, after swimming until we shivered with cold, we'd warm up on the turquoise mezzanine, eating frozen Mars bars in the sun.

But mostly I remember the library. Rows of bookcases, two shelves each, filled with picture books that smelled of must and ink and glue. Every week, carrying a new clutch of books under my arm, I balanced atop the concrete wall outside the library, holding my mother's hand.

When I think of the library, it is always summer. I am lying with my belly against the cool linoleum floor, propped on my elbows with a book spread open before me. In that season when the world of home wobbled on its axis, an orderly, multihued universe turned between those hard, cloth-bound covers. A cosmos far beyond the straw-colored streets of Hays.

That night, in the Tea Rose Inn, I felt spent. Bruised. I'd been on the road for eleven days, checking houses and addresses off my list, touring museums, walking neighborhoods and small-town streets, soaking things up, taking them in. Even veering off the road to read historical markers.

I thought it was only fatigue. As much as I wanted to ignore it, the exhaustion that had dogged me since Denver was now dragging behind me like an anchor. A side effect of the radiation for cancer, it made even breathing feel like an act of will. Long before dark, supperless and cranky, I crawled under the covers and slept like the dead. The next morning, I dragged myself to breakfast, where chipper Debbie and Jerry, who'd stayed in the Peacock Room down the hall, announced their lifetime goal of visiting every national park. I thought to myself, why not visit every roadside historical marker while you're at it? But that was me. I was the one on an endless road of markers, maps, road signs, schools, museums, houses, and towns. Driving and driving and driving. And why?

For the first time since leaving San Francisco, I wanted to go home. To walk city streets filled with other people walking, checking out shop windows, soaking up the neighborhoods—each with its own face and mood. Or hop on a bus to Macy's and rifle the discount racks. Or sit in a café, sip a cup of chai, and watch the urban circus.

Hear the car horns, bus brakes, hustle and jive, radios sauntering down the avenue.

A week ago, I'd wanted to learn everything I could about Kansas. Now Hays's history museum felt like too much work. So did old Fort Hays. Bill Cody, Hickok, Custer—they'd all been headquartered there. But who needed it? I didn't know that the fort was haunted by the ghost of Elizabeth Polly, dead of cholera in 1867. People swear they've seen her in her sunbonnet and long blue dress, wandering the hill above the fort. Maybe I would have seen her, if I'd only known. I seemed to have a talent for ghosts.

Instead, I spent my last morning wandering the Fort Hays State campus, pelted by freezing drizzle, searching for the band shell, which Tara thought had been there. Nobody knew anything about it. I spent an hour digging into the only past I had the heart for—fossils in glass boxes, animatronic dinosaurs, and the Cretaceous sea display at the Sternberg Museum of Natural History.

"Here in Kansas, listeners, it's forty-five degrees. Rain promises to be with us for the next five days, relieved by periods of drizzle. Enjoy it while it lasts. Cause winter's just around the corner!"

I drove east toward Wichita in a thick drizzle, spray smearing the windshield. Every little town looked like every other little town I'd seen for the past week—cookie-cutter commas in the long, droning sentence of wheat, wheat, wheat, wheat, corn. The same signs in every town. "The Churches of Wherever Welcome You!" "Nameless Town, Home of the Whatever!" "Go, Fighting Animal Name or Warrior Tribe!"

Near Victoria, a few miles outside of Hays, St. Fidelis, "the Cathedral of the Plains," loomed over the horizon. Its Romanesque spires and rose window grew enormous as I drew near, like a vision of absurdity in the center of a vast emptiness. And it was only one of three huge German Catholic churches in the space of only a few miles.

I stopped in just to say that I had. The place had pews enough for a thousand people. The early German parishioners' optimism seemed as quixotic as the martyred St. Fidelis, who was murdered while saying mass in 1622 by the Calvinists he'd set out to save.

A week earlier, I would have loved it. The hopefulness, the ambition, the expectation of a miracle. I would have loved the stone, the rose window, the filigreed metal crosses in the cemetery. I would have loved the fact that all these centuries later, St. Fidelis's Capuchin brothers occupied the rectory.

Now, it seemed as mad as my journey. Who would want to live in such a godforsaken place? How many people showed up for mass here? Five?

West of Salina, close to meltdown, I snarled at myself, "Why the hell does it matter where you used to live?"

How easily I can forget the lessons of the meditation cushion. If I'd sat down, breathed in, and looked, tasted the raisin of this ugly day, I would have seen that under my fatigue lay anger, and under anger lay grief. Yes, I'd finally taken my long-envisioned journey, revisiting family sites. But for nearly two weeks, I had also been traveling the geography of loss. At every house, in every town, I had regathered the weight of all the losses, all the shocks and jolts of family crises, all the grief from all the moving. Grief that reached across the decades to touch more recent sorrows. The loss of the Victorian house and P still wafted in and out of my days. Just before my trip, I'd spent the weeks settling into yet another new home, painting walls, making curtains, spinning out those tenuous threads of new connection that would make the place feel like home. My body, fatigued and compromised, so recently made mortal, offered its own reasons for grief.

I must have sensed, too, that it was time to move on, to let go my hold on these images—the lost school windows, a schoolyard fence, a dark tree—to free them from their museum of hurts and release them into the flux of time. And I needed to let my body rest, to be still for a while.

As I had all my life, I needed a warm place to hunker down.

....

CHAPTER FIVE

Wichita Vortex Redux

"Hey, hey! You're here!"

I could hear her Cheshire grin over the phone, her voice big enough for the stage.

The year I turned eight, Charla became Tara's and my best friend, and our spree of slumber parties, popcorn, and carryings on lasted for the next five years. At the start of eighth grade, when Tara and I got scholarships to Collegiate prep, our orbits began to drift. We became bookish at Collegiate; and Charla became a star, playing jazz piano at South High, singing in musicals, designing sets and costumes. By the time we graduated, her family had moved to the new west-side burbs. But we'd never lost each other, and Charla's voice felt like home.

"Do you need directions?"

"I'll figure it out," I said. "I've got a map." Charla laughed.

I was lost in my own hometown.

South Seneca should have been easy; it runs like a river through the south side, where I'd lived for ten years. But when I exited the freeway, the neighborhood seemed surreal, the street names and intersections calling from the far side of a half-remembered dream.

I pulled off on a side street and draped a map over the steering wheel. It was the first Wichita map I think I'd ever seen. Before, I hadn't needed one. My well-worn paths had led from house to school, school to Scouts, to and from Charla's house, the rec center, work, the pool. I hadn't needed a map even when I'd learned to drive. Turn right at the mailbox, left at the yard with the flowering plum, cross the bridge, follow the river to the second light.

On the map, I traced our daily route to high school across the class and race lines that divided the city. Starting from our white, lower-middle-class enclave on the south side, my finger made its way along the Arkansas; across the Douglas Street Bridge; and into the glass, steel, and limestone canyon of downtown. Every week day for five years, we then zigzagged Douglas to Hydraulic to Central to Grove, turned left at Tenth into the black ghetto, where we dropped Mom off at Ingalls Elementary. Then we turned right at Thirteenth and, in another ten blocks, headed into money. Past streets with names like Stratford and Pinecrest, houses with game rooms and swimming pools, nineteenth-century mansions of red brick or stone, homes of the well-off and wealthy, where classmates threw parties and game nights and breakfasts after prom. Then we kept driving. Past the Art Association and Cessna to where the buildings petered out and the country clubs and countryside began. Forty-five minutes and four worlds from home, we turned into Collegiate's parking lot. South-side girls at the rich kids' school.

Tara and I couldn't afford ski trips to Vail. To help pay our tuition, we cleaned chalkboards after school. When the child support never came, Mom took a second job in retail, selling upscale women's fashions to keep us in our house and hockey uniforms. But our friends never sneered about neighborhoods or money, and we had affluent résumés: newspaper, honor roll, pep club, lit mag, yearbook, debate, class president. In different years, we each won the Headmaster's Award. And we also knew we weren't poor. Poor was the kids my mother taught who showed up in the morning hungry.

My mother taught me a lot about crossing boundaries. When she started at Ingalls in 1964, ten years after *Brown v. Board of Education*, Wichita was still resisting desegregation. The school board dragged its feet and realtors guarded neighborhood color lines throughout that decade and into the next. The NAACP filed lawsuits, school board meetings filled with rage, and the city threatened to close black schools. My mother, who hated confrontation and avoided the fray, still made her position clear. She could have requested reassignment to a different, white, school, but she didn't want to. At a time when plenty of white people still called her school's neighborhood "nigger town," she hugged her black students and loved her black colleagues, fed her hungry kids and befriended many parents. In 1971, when the courts threatened the still-segregated Wichita schools with the loss of federal funding, she convinced many of our neighbors' children to volunteer for cross-busing.

I was still in grade school in the sixties, too young to take to the streets. But watching the civil rights struggle on TV taught me how much courage justice demands; I liked to think that if I were old enough, I'd take up my sign and march, too. What I saw on the news taught me that people didn't have to stay where they were told to. And my mother showed me that people on both sides of a wall could help to tear it down.

I folded the map, ready to explore. The south side, always modest, had turned mangy around the edges. Ugly little houses, nasty little strip malls, and strangled vegetation lined Seneca Street. Then fast-food joints and discount stores, the Payless Shoes that Shannon managed for a while, and finally, the Westway Shopping Center. It looked depressed, the parking lot half empty. I cruised past the shops, looking for the movie house where I got my first job. Age fifteen, a dollar an hour. Illegal on both counts, which seemed to give me some measure of immunity. The first time I carded a kid for an R-rated movie, I was so flustered by his blond hair and leather jacket that I couldn't locate the birth date on his driver's license and, when I did, couldn't do the math. I never checked IDs again. The manager didn't seem to mind. Another time, I went into the projection booth and flipped the sound switch so I could listen to the movie, something stupid and grisly about cannibals, with shrunken heads on sticks. So I flipped off the switch and went back to the popcorn counter. A few minutes later, a man came out of the theater to complain. Someone had shut off the volume. Oops. The manager shrugged.

You'd think my biggest blunder might have nudged him a little. I was scooping a yellow glop of fat from a five-gallon tub into the popcorn popper, when my foot, unbeknownst to me, hit the silent alarm. A few minutes later, I was leaning on the glass counter filled with Jujubes and Junior Mints, getting high on the smell of "Fresh! Hot!" popping corn, when a sheriff's officer clutching a rifle streaked past the glass front door. Hmm, I thought, that's odd. His face flashed into the door frame then vanished. I stared at where he'd been. Face flash. The door jerked open and he slipped inside, back to the wall, rifle tight in both hands. He was breathing hard, pumped up on adrenalin. I stared at him from behind the candy counter. "Everything all right?" he asked. Yeah, I nodded. He looked at me as if to ask where the gunman was hiding, the one forcing me to lie. The sheriff looked for him behind the counter and inside the projection booth but came up empty. At last, he exhaled. He seemed a little put out. "Look," he said, "let me show you the trip lever." Right along the baseboard beneath the ticket machine. I was mortified. Still, what idiot would put an alarm right where the ticket seller puts her feet?

The manager only said, "Oh yeah, you gotta watch out for that thing." For a dollar an hour, he wasn't about to be choosy. The minute I turned sixteen, I got a proper job scooping ice cream at the Colonial Ice Cream Parlor in a nicer part of town. It paid $1.35 an hour plus tips and a free scoop every shift.

The movie dive was gone. So was the big GEM, a discount store where my mom bought us hot caramel corn in paper cones (the popcorn theme continues). I'd hoped for a café to sit at and soak up the atmosphere, but Westway had clearly never become a café sort of place.

My father had once driven with me through the same parking

lot on some errand or other. We'd stopped for a pedestrian, and as the woman crossed in front of our car, she yawned. "You bore me, too, baby," my father said, loud enough for her to hear. For a second my blood stopped. Then I folded up that little tidbit and dropped it through the slot labeled "Facts about the Person Who Is My Father." I couldn't have been more than ten, but I could parse the moment. He had taken the yawn of a woman he'd never met as a personal insult. Later, I would see its sexual import. Any woman immune to his charms earned his angry rejection.

A few blocks from GEM, St. Anne's church had been spared the south-side leprosy. That's where, looking like a tiny bride in white lace and veil, I had made my first Communion. But I was a not-very-spiritual, fidgety child. On Sundays before mass began, while Tara and my mother prayed on their knees, I prepared by sticking my fingers into the hymnal at the pages announced on the song board. While mass droned on, I ached for any chance to belt out a hymn.

Besides the fidgeting and the singing, my most vivid St. Anne's memories include blond-colored pews and the twin teenage girls who showed up every Sunday. They had matching turned-up noses and pulled-up top lips, like when you push the tip of your nose up with your finger and your lip just follows along. I couldn't not stare at the doubleness of it all. The twice turned-up nostrils, the two lifted lips, the twin pairs of teeth peeking out rabbitlike, ready for carrots.

A block from the church, the round building that molted every spring into a different theme restaurant or nightclub had become the Circle Cinema XXX. The Kingsborough Apartments still sprawled across ten acres of asphalt parking lot, now cracked and chipped with divots. At eighteen Shannon had moved in there, three blocks from Payless, five blocks from home. She had bailed on Collegiate and walked out of South High. By the time I moved to Austin in 1979, she was nineteen and sliding toward Payless-for-life on the south side. A year later, on a whim, I invited her to move in with me and my husband and two little girls in Texas. In our nine hundred square feet of graduate student splendor. It felt like the beginning of amends for her being neglected, for our absence from each other as children. She took the next train out of Dodge.

For all the south side's demerits, we'd also met Charla there. In our fourth-grade year, more times than I could count, I raced my bike from our house on Bennett to her house on Martinson, down the street and over the foot bridge, five blocks away. Each time, her mother greeted me, "Wow! You flew!" Everything was better at Charla's. We ate popcorn from a giant yellow pottery bowl pocked with craters and drank delicious cups of Tang, a beverage my mother pooh-poohed. The Sandersons had a black-and-white kitten, Mighty Mouse, named after a cartoon superhero. We had a cat, Gravy, named after food. Charla had Barbies. My mother hated Barbies. Of course, Charla probably thought our house was better than hers—what kid doesn't prefer the novelty of other kids' snacks and toys?

Over the years, her Easy-Bake Oven gave way to Monopoly marathons and triple solitaire. We tap-danced together and played in the school band, sometimes swapping instruments, my clarinet for her flute, sometimes swapping strep throat. The three of us refined the art of staying up all night without bringing Charla's bleary-eyed mother to the door at two o'clock in the morning to shut the party down. In the morning, Tara and I staggered home with bags under our eyes and syrup-drenched pancakes in our bellies, all washed down with a big plastic cup full of Tang.

For a while our two families were upwardly mobile together. In the summer between our fourth and fifth grades, my father now worked the news desk and the Sandersons could afford a bigger house. So we all moved into the same new development, half a block apart. Within a year, hallelujah, my parents built the house on Magnolia, right next door to Charla's.

That's the Charla house I remember best. Next-door nirvana. Unlike mine, Charla's mother Ruth stayed home and baked, gardened, cleaned, sewed, and saved money. She shopped with coupons, stretched the milk supply by adding powdered milk and water, and drove across town to buy baked beans by the case on sale. She'd inherited frugality from her parents, German Lutheran farmers. Ruth even kept her long hair pinned up in a big, loopy German-lady bun. She wore oversized glasses and laughed a lot and, sometimes for dessert, whipped Jell-O so full of bubbles it turned into pink sugar foam.

Best of all, theirs was a house of art. Paintings and weavings hung on walls, sculptures stood in the yard, and everything from mashed potatoes to pancake syrup came to the table in hand-thrown pots. Nearly every piece had come by way of barter, traded for one of Charlie's watercolors.

Charla's father Charlie painted Kansas landscapes, not as a regional hobbyist might, with heartfelt dabs of color, but as a genuine artist who happened to paint the place he lived. He knew the thousand moods of the Kansas sky, the tempers of the grass. The loneliness of a windmill or the late-fall light filtered through a windbreak. In our house a moody blue wooded creek bank in fog hung above the couch, which we'd traded for with one of my father's hand-woven chairs. I felt proud that the chair had measured up to such a painting. My father usually couldn't compare.

Charlie's basement studio seemed halo lit, the brushes, paints, textured paper, tables, easels, and mat board shining with promise. While we ran in and out of the studio, Ruth helped with framing and packing up for art shows; and they both let us hang around to watch. Charlie showed us all kinds of paint tricks. Shake salt onto just-painted light blue wash, and faint starbursts appear, an icy winter sky flecked with light.

When he wasn't teaching painting at South High, Charlie was home, a steady, playful father. He poked fun in a way that said, "I see you, I like you, let's be silly." When we showed up at lunch wearing our latest eye shadow experiments, he made us feel noticed and charming and lovingly joshed. "Oh, my," he'd say, making much of the new look. "How'd you get your black eye?"

I wanted Ruth and Charlie for my own. Competent, at ease with the world. They worked hard—Charlie at school, Ruth at home, both of them in the studio. But unlike my parents, they seemed comfortable together, sure of each other. They knew how to send down roots and flourish where they were. And like real Kansans, they could make anything, from tree houses to gardens.

Ruth's summer garden took up their whole backyard—strawberries, cherries, carrots, green beans, tomatoes, radishes, sunflowers, zucchini. Every leaf pumped up with Miracle-Gro. By July that Kansas garden had greened up like a rain forest in the hazy heat. There, amid the green beans, all was right with the world. One summer night, Tara, Charla, and I slept on cots on the Sanderson's screened-in porch; in the morning, the sun rose burning red through the trees at the edge of the yard. The garden started to steam and buzz, bees bobbled into squash blossoms, birds chittered in the trees. On the porch tiny black ants streamed single file out of the drainpipe as though they'd been sent for, hoisted up our Oreo crumbs, and carried them away.

It was hot midsummer the day my father left. We'd just returned from a tension-wracked trip to California—Dad's final, failed try at Hollywood. The tv anchor job must have ended around that time, too—the failures mounting. That morning, my mother set a neat pile of his clean white T-shirts by the front door and shot him a withering look. I'd never seen her angry. Not at him. I was pretty sure I knew what it meant.

On the last night of our vacation, a few hours from Wichita we'd stopped at a diner so my father could get a cup of coffee. He went in while the rest of us waited, wrapped in the hush that happens when the road drone stops and the engine ticks down to cool. From Los Angeles, across the desert, across the Rockies, across the High Plains, we'd been in the car for days. My sisters may have been asleep, but my mother sat silently awake in the front seat. Dad sat at the counter with his back to the window. The waitress smiled, poured a hot cup, and set it down in front of him. He lit a cigarette and exhaled, the smoke curling up and fanning out along the ceiling lights. He leaned on one forearm; lifted the cigarette with his other hand; and cocking his head, took a long, slow drag. I knew he'd be squinting. Exhale. He parked the cigarette on the dimpled rim of the ashtray. Sipped his coffee. He seemed to be taking his time, feeling his freedom. Finally, he stubbed the cigarette into the ashtray and drained the cup. He paid at the register, thumbed a coin tip from his palm onto the counter, and came out into the dark. When he opened the car door, the dome light cast quiet shadows over my mother's unmoving face. Settling into the seat, he took a deep breath, sighed, switched on the ignition, and said, "Last leg."

Last leg of the trip, last leg of the marriage, last leg of life even as we had known it. I heard the multivalence of his meaning, and I knew he heard it, too. The question caught in my throat, "When are you going to tell us about the divorce?"

Everyone but Shannon already knew. Even before we'd left Kansas weeks earlier, Mom had confided in Tara. Dad was having another affair, this time with a woman in his current play; and Mom had had enough. That she saw fit to disclose this to a child deserves a moment's pause. But Tara kept her secret, even when we stopped at our cousins' in Arizona and, for more than a week, shot pool, swam, and ate quesadillas at the mall while Dad went on to Hollywood.

I sussed it out later, after we joined Dad in California. At the beach, I overheard my mother talking with my aunt Colleen. I kept the secret, too. But once we were back in Wichita, when my mother laid those folded white T-shirts on the living room step, I flushed her into the open. "Mom, why are you doing that?" Then they told us.

That afternoon, Tara, Shannon, and I went stunned, mute, and swollen-eyed to a watermelon party in Charla's garden. Ruth carved the watermelon and kept up a cheerful chatter. Charla and her brother Joel chased around, trying to trip each other, laughing. Shannon sat alone on a picnic bench looking fragile and small, her white tennis shoes not quite reaching the ground, her straight, blond bangs falling across her eyes. Within weeks she would try to hang herself from the basement rafters. I stared at the leaky slab on my paper plate and picked at the seeds with my fork. But after a while I felt better. At least for Tara and me, whatever else happened, I knew that Charla's house would hold us and hold us steady.

Charlie died first, in 1993, and Ruth not long after. I wanted to see their house again, and ours next door. But two blocks away, too exhausted to give the moment thoughtful attention, I turned around. I needed rest. I wanted to turn where I had as a child, to Charla's house. But not the old one, one that could hold me in real time. She lived on the west side now, in the house Ruth and Charlie had bought when we were sixteen. I had to look at the map to find it.

I woke up the next morning in the Black-and-White Room hung over. Charla and I had celebrated with champagne and red wine and more wine and a marathon game of "Remember that? Remember them?" Charla's husband Chris had endured it for a while, then rolled his eyes and went searching for Alex, his cat.

For most of the day, with Chris and Charla gone to work, I loafed in my pj's, recovering from the road, waiting out the rain. How good it was to be still, to be held by the quiet of this house. I wandered. Completely familiar and entirely changed, it was still an artist's house. I recognized some of Ruth and Charlie's things, but Chris and Charla had added dozens of pieces. Prints and drawings in my room; Charla's antique costumes—a silk kimono, a lace Victorian bodice—hanging on peacock blue walls in what Charla now called the "dressing room"; several of Charlie's large landscapes in the living room and over the staircase; and, throughout the house, etchings, pottery, sculpture, oils, watercolors, fiber art, landscapes, abstracts, figures, and Ruth's bevy of blown-glass paperweights. Nearly everything was local.

Yes, Virginia, there are artists in Kansas. How completely I'd forgotten. A painter had lived next door, my father had acted in a downtown theater, and we'd trailed Charla through museums and galleries. But when I left Kansas at seventeen, I'd packed none of that in my Kansas portmanteau. I'd already bought into the fable of cultural aridity. Now I stared at a Lisa Grossman sunset until I longed for one of my own.

One morning in 1965, Wichitans woke to find this declaration on the front page of the *Eagle and Beacon*: "Wichita imposes a dark night on the soul of its youth." The pundit was Allen Ginsberg. The city, he said, was actually "a garden of Eden. . . . Because Wichita had produced more than its share of Beats—Michael McClure, Roxie Powell, Bruce Connor, J. Richard White, Stan Brakhage, Robert Branaman and Charlie Plymell. But officially, it's a wasteland." Every artist he named had fled.

Ginsberg's comments, one of many in his front-page interview, marked the last act of a drama that had started the year before at Moody Connell's Skidrow Beanery.

Moody had opened the Beanery for "the bums" on Wichita's East Douglas, which by the sixties had declined from Second Empire elegance to American urban blight. A block from the once-posh Eaton Hotel—then a derelict sro—the Beanery offered "Okie T-bone (toast and creamed gravy)" for fifteen cents; "Pea-farm [prison farm] Steak (baloney, fries, onions, bread, and beans)" for a quarter; and "Jail House Chili" for that same twenty-five-cent bargain price. Everything came with beans. But then the city shut the Beanery down. Officials cited thirty-seven code violations, though everyone, including the press, knew the real crime was poetry.

Moody had gotten ambitious, adding folk music and readings to his menu and, along with works by Plymell and Ferlinghetti, selling Ginsberg's *Howl*. High school and college kids crowded in for the music and poetry and for the "scene"; and though Moody didn't serve alcohol, Lieutenant Colonel J. H. Reeves claimed he was selling "obscene trash" as literature. Of course, Officer Reeves hadn't read the books, but no matter. After months of surveillance, harassment, and skirmishes in the press, Moody lost the Beanery and became a cause.

Readers flooded the paper with letters supporting Moody. Ginsberg weighed in, demanding to know why the mayor, citizens, and university faculty weren't fighting for "such a crucial constitutional matter as freedom of expression. . . . Is Nobody home in Wichita?"

Ginsberg would trouble Wichita's conscience again the following year, when the Beanery reopened as the Vortex Gallery with the bard as the main event. His antiwar epic "Wichita Vortex Sutra" takes aim at the city he'd come to chastise. Wichita,

Vortex

of telephone radio aircraft assembly frame ammunition
petroleum nightclub Newspaper streets illuminated by Bright
EMPTINESS—

It also describes Ginsberg's mixed Wichita reception, torn by young people hungry for truth and by an establishment filled with indignation.

> On to Wichita to prophesy! O frightful Bard!
> into the heart of the Vortex
> where anxiety rings
> the University with millionaire pressure,
> lonely crank telephone voices sighing in dread,
> and students waken trembling in their beds
> with dreams of a new truth warm as meat.

The vice squad steered clear of the Vortex opening but showed up the next night, when Ginsberg, along with Plymell and others, read at a local hangout. Young officers, not sure if they should arrest the poets, confiscated a manuscript and read it over the radio to their superiors. Ginsberg must have relished the scene,

> Police dumbfounded leaning on
> > their radiocar hoods
> While Poets chant to Allah in the roadhouse Showboat!

While the cops awaited their orders, Ginsberg railed against censorship and rallied legal muscle. Finally, more-experienced officers arrived and let the show go on.

The following week, Ginsberg's interview appeared in the paper. At the time, he may have been right about official Wichita's dark night. Growing up there, at least, I'd adopted that view as my own. How could a kid stand it? How soon could I leave?

Of course, Wichita was hardly the only outpost of intolerance in the sixties. Police in New York had seized *Howl* and tried it for obscenity just ten years before. After raids on the New York Beat joints drove the artists to San Francisco in 1957, San Francisco also put *Howl* on trial. Kansas hasn't been on the cutting edge of much in recent decades; true to form, its condemnation of the Beats came a little behind the times.

Still, the story of Moody's confirms many people's view of Kansas as emblem of the reactionary and provincial. During the decades I'd been away, "many people" had included me.

Things haven't always been so. Whitman praised the state that Ginsberg vilified. He sang of the

> Chants going forth from the centre, from Kansas, and
> > thence, equidistant,
> Shooting in pulses of fire, ceaseless, to vivify all.

Kansas electric, heart of a region Whitman called "the vast Something." After his Kansas trip in 1879, he proclaimed the prairie

A newer garden of creation . . .

. . . .

The crown and teeming paradise, so far, of time's
accumulations.

Times change, meanings change. Kansas has been, at various times, "a place of abundance," "The Great American Desert," the Garden State, and "Bleeding Kansas," proving ground of the Civil War. When it rejected slavery in 1861, it became a national moral beacon that remained lit for decades. In the 1890s, populist, progressive Kansas enacted corporate and railroad reform that broke monopolies and regulated tariffs. In 1912 it granted women's suffrage, seven years before the nation would follow suit. The first state to institute direct primaries and the direct election of senators, it sent "Sockless" Jerry Simpson to Washington as congressman from the People's Party. In 1916, 16 percent of the state voted for Socialist Party candidate Eugene Debs, and the debate topic of the Goodland literary society was "Resolved, that capitalism is the direct cause of more poverty than intoxicating liquor." Kansas led so often in populist reform, worker protection, and social welfare that William Allen White, Kansas's renowned journalist, could write in 1922 that "Kansas is the Mother Shipton, the Madame Thebes, the Witch of Endor. . . . When anything is going to happen in this country, it happens first in Kansas. . . . Kansas is hardly a state. It is a kind of prophecy!"

Lest we conclude that Kansas was its own best admirer, a New York Times editorial had judged in 1921 that "Nothing too good can be said of Kansas and her dreams." It was meant unambiguously. Until the late 1920s, the state held its position as a national star.

Much of that history has been forgotten or never been learned, even by people who live there. Or people like me who left and looked back sneering. For most of us, Kansas's character has long been mired where it foundered in the twenties and thirties. First, its agrarian promise blew away in the Dust Bowl, along with millions of acres of topsoil. Then while the country urbanized, the state kept farming wheat; and when the federal government repealed Prohibition in 1933, Kansas refused to fall off the wagon. It remained dry until 1978. By then, I'd been suckin' down Lone Stars in Texas for nearly four years, and Kansas bashing had long been a national sport. Perhaps because it had ridden so high for so long, Kansas—more than its neighbors like Iowa—had become the quintessential whipping state, icon of the ignorant, moralistic, and unwashed. On the national scene, Kansas had become irrelevant.

Then it became Auntie Em's farm. *The Wizard of Oz* hit the small screen in 1956, and in 1959 it became an annual television rite. Every October (or was it April?), my sisters and I settled in with our popcorn and pajamas to watch what we'd learned by heart, Dorothy running from the horrid Miss Gulch, Toto popping out of the basket, both of them whirling from boring drabness to a munchkin-filled and Technicolor world.

The Wizard of Oz is the only cultural geography lesson many people have ever learned about Kansas. They're quite sure the state's little more than a dust-bowl farm in a flat, black-and-white world. Even now, when I tell them I grew up in Kansas, one out of ten will ask "How's Auntie Em?" and the rest will ask after Toto.

In Wichita at Charla's, I began to challenge my own Oz version of Kansas, or the place began to challenge it for me. The more Kansas opened my eyes, the more I thought of the six blind men's accounts of the elephant. No single one describes the whole, and some are outright lies. In the nineteenth-century, when land speculators and railroads dropped pamphlets as far as the Russian steppes to recruit settlers for Kansas, the new Eden, they left out a few details. Like grasshoppers and prairie fires and dugouts, holes in the ground you might live in for your first year or five on the prairie. The year Whitman rhapsodized about Kansas, the state was suffering the worst drought in its recorded history. And people who drive through a strip of Kansas four lanes wide declare the whole state to be flat.

In my trips back to Kansas over the next few years, I would take to disproving those rumors of flatness by getting off the interstate. The high plains of western Kansas are flat. So are the Arkansas River lowlands. In a recent cheeky study, researchers, taking their sample just outside of Wichita, concluded that Kansas was, indeed, flatter than a pancake. But off the interstate and out of the lowlands, I found a different Kansas. The Blue Hills and Smoky Hill uplands, the Flint Hills, the southeastern Kansas Ozarks, the northeastern glacier fields, the south central Red Hills and Cimarron Breaks—not flat.

But the more I collected evidence of variations and contours and elevations, I began to think, so what? What if the entire state really were flatter than a pancake? Can't that be beautiful? What's with our landscape fetish for the vertical and verdant, the grandly picturesque, or Romantically sublime? Or is it simply that anything stamped "Kansas" must automatically be mocked?

Stereotypes, rumors, limited views. We all take parts for wholes. The trunk of the elephant. The ear. Why do people remember Toto but not that *Brown v. Board of Education* started in Topeka? Why do they remember "Wichita Vortex Sutra" but not that without Wichita the Beats would be four guys sitting around Café Vesuvio in San Francisco's North Beach? Why not know that, three blocks from where the Beanery would open and six years before it closed, young African Americans staged the first successful lunch counter sit-in in the country? In four weeks they brought the Dockum Drugstore chain to its knees, forcing it to serve everyone throughout the state, regardless of color. That was 1958, two years before Greensboro. But who remembers?

Kansas does tend to retry the *Scopes* trial during school board elections, and the media is quick to pounce. But the majority of Kansans cheered when the 2006 election returned education to science. In 2006 the Ulrich Gallery at Wichita State hosted a show of Beat visual arts. And when I last checked Wichita's entertainment calendar, Margaret Cho was in town.

I hadn't worked all this out during my week in Wichita. But lounging at Charla's, surrounded by art, something started to change. I knew the global culturati rarely come calling. Who'd imagine finding the next big thing up here in Toto's hayloft? Still, a mischievous light peeked around the corner of my blinders. Art happened with or without the critics' imprimatur. It happened even here.

Chris and Charla sometimes talk of leaving. They're tired of some Kansans saying, when they think something's a little too artsy or arcane, "well, la-di-da." But I think that's just the defensiveness of the long– and often–laughed at, of folks who know they register in the coastal consciousness as hicks and hayseeds. But are Kansans any more provincial than my friend who lives on the Upper West Side and says she could never live anywhere else? Never? Anywhere? Or the New York painter who guffawed when I mentioned artists in Kansas? Or the man I met in Santa Monica who doesn't see the point of going anywhere else—not Paris or Morocco or even Los Angeles, which is ten minutes away? Or the San Francisco hipster who'll converse with you over a glass of Sonoma merlot, unless you vote Republican?

Are Kansans more provincial than the masses who denounce the flyover zone as a waste of time and petro fuel? From my current vantage point, to all of you I say, jump out of your jumbo jet, and see what's on the ground. From thirty-five thousand feet, even Michelangelo has the brain of a gnat.

I decided to dive out of my own dirigible. On my third day in Wichita, temperatures hovered just above freezing, and the intermittent drizzle had become an unrelenting drag. I'd come to visit old houses, old parks, old schools; but they didn't seem so much to matter. I'd spent the previous evening at a gallery opening with Charla meeting musicians and painters. Seeing old haunts seemed less exciting than seeing something I didn't already know. I decided to drive north to Lindsborg.

After two days of loafing, the road felt friendly again. I settled in behind the metronomic rhythm of the wipers and the womblike murmur of the rain. Kansas spread out before me on the wet bourn of winter—a lowering sky, bright green fields of new winter wheat, dark soil drinking in the rain. Traveling along in our windowed cocoons, the semi drivers and I shared the solidarity of being out in the weather, like sailors on heavy seas.

Lindsborg, built by immigrant Swedes, still wears red wooden shutters on its windows and still serves lacy pancakes with lingonberry jam. I couldn't wait to get my fork into those. But even more, I wanted to see the work of Birger Sandzén and Lester Raymer, who had turned Lindsborg into an artists' haven.

Sandzén arrived from Sweden in 1894 at the age of twenty-three. He'd studied painting at home and in Paris, at the studio of French symbolist Aman-Jean. He could have made a superb career in Europe. But Sandzén chose Lindsborg, where he taught French and art at Bethany College for fifty-two years. On a mission to bring Kansans to art, he organized art clubs and exhibitions, talked and cajoled and founded the Prairie Printmakers and Prairie Watercolor Painters Association. In his non-teaching hours, he drew, etched, made woodblocks, linocuts, and lithographs, and painted in watercolors and oils. Exhibitions throughout the country, including two highly acclaimed shows in New York, brought invitations to teach and paint in more prestigious places. Yet, though he spent many summers painting in the Rockies or teaching in larger cities, Sandzén always came back to Lindsborg. During his first New York show, he even stayed in Lindsborg to teach. He also made so many copies of most of his prints and gave so many away—refusing to make them a rarity—that he had no idea who had them all.

In the Sandzén gallery, a small brick building with linoleum floors, I was the only visitor. I studied Sandzén's paintings, his Cezanne-like attention to structures and planes, the fauve palette of his landscapes. In his pointillist-inspired *Twilight*, a Kansas sky hung ripe in pomegranate, purples, and greens. It seemed entirely right. Sandzén had captured the play of color and light at prairie dusk, the motion of air and clouds. Many of his works depicted the Rockies, which he loved. But his Kansas works, which he often drew and painted along the Smoky Hill River or Wild Horse Creek, seemed more intimate. Undaunted by broad, mountainless spaces, Sandzén painted them close-up—a tree, a river bank, a cabin—as though he knew them like a friend.

Lester Raymer, Lindsborg's second resident spirit, arrived in 1945 with a magic art box full of treasures. In love with the circus; schooled in the Bible; and inspired by El Greco, Russian iconography, commedia dell'arte, and a farmer father who could make anything "out of nothing"—Raymer filled his Red Barn Studio with wizardry. Sally Johnson, a docent and painter, led me around the studio, which Raymer had cobbled together from an old hotel laundry and barn turned carriage house. It teemed with his paintings, drawings, furniture, carvings, prints, pottery, sculpture, banners, and toys. Everything from Byzantine crosses and sandstone saints to fantastic roosters crafted from wire or candelabra and crosses made of snipped tin cans. Terra-cotta Madonnas and a miniature four-horse carousel. A modernist clay St. Francis, a medieval cement St. Gerome, and a child's Noah's ark—replete with hand-carved animals in pairs.

Sally lifted lids and latches on cabinets and chests, pointing out Raymer's wrought-iron locks and adornments. Raymer was a genius technician; even up close, it's hard to tell that Noah's ark is roofed with corrugated cardboard. That some of his exquisite creations— candelabra, chandeliers, jewelry boxes—had been made from tin can lids or papier-mâché.

Growing up with Charla, whenever we walked through the TG&Y fingering the toys or, later, through Macy's trying on clothes, Charla would say, "We could make that." We often did. Among other things, we built apartments for our troll dolls out of Girl Scout cookie cartons, hanging blue corduroy wallpaper and gluing together matchbox chairs.

Best of all, from a pink rectangular eraser, Charla created Eraser Baby. She carved a straight mouth and pinprick eyes on the eraser's flat face, glued on bits of sponge for arms and legs, and attached yellow yarn hair. Then we launched Eraser Baby's fashion line: a pleated skirt, a flannel shift, a yellow-feathered headdress. From office garb to glitter, an inch and a half long. Eraser Baby and her wardrobe now lie tucked away in a Whitman's Sampler box. I also still come home from shopping with nothing but the conviction that whatever I saw and wanted, I could make.

Raymer's workshop vibrated with the spirit of a child who could say of every toy she longed for, "We could make that." And who, like Raymer, could make anything out of nothing. In part, it was the frugality of making do. But as Eraser Baby always reminds me, making do can also lead to making wonders.

I spent the rest of the afternoon gallery hopping. First, the Small World Gallery to see Steven Scott's grain elevators and David Hiltner's stoneware jars. I'd met David, a potter, at the gallery opening the night before; his large dark jars were textured like plow furrows, with tiny grain silos standing on the lids. The oblique geometries of Scott's graphic elevators stood out in bright pastels and neons. Both artists, like Sandzén, had been unembarrassed to honor Kansas with the exacting attention of an artist's eye. Maybe, I thought, I could make something from it, too.

Down the street, in her studio, I met Elizabeth Walker, who wove hand-spun, hand-dyed threads into jackets and shawls. I wanted one of everything. I fingered a long, soft wrap of silky dark reds and peacock blue, the supple threads suffused with light. I could never have made it myself. Since then, I've worn my wrap to San Francisco dinner parties, film festival openings, white-tablecloth restaurants, and an American Conservatory Theater production of Edward Albee's *The Goat.* I love wearing Kansas art in California. It feels subversive, like smuggling contraband.

Once back in Wichita, I spent Sunday in Charla's studio, where Charlie used to paint, helping make costumes for an upcoming Christmas performance of *Hansel and Gretel.* While Charla laid out and cut fabric, I glued silver holly sprigs and berries on tinselly tiaras—headpieces for winter fairies. I burned the hell out of my fingers with the glue gun. But it felt like old times.

Except for our thirteenth house, on Magnolia Street, no address on my list felt pressing or powerfully charged. Maybe because I'd been older in Wichita, lived there longer, left because I'd wanted to. I'd also taken away whole chapters of recollection, not a handful of luminous, aching fragments as I had from Goodland or Hays. Besides, Kansas—at last—was becoming bigger than my past.

Dutifully, I rolled by my schools to check them off my dance card. All three of my elementary schools had lost their portable buildings; the baby boom was over. Truesdell Junior High looked sprawling as ever, though less scary. In the seventh grade, I'd discovered my capacity for cruelty. A short, schlubby girl whose name I don't remember began following me around like a puppy, wanting to be friends. For a few weeks, I made her my pet, sat with her at lunch, flattered her. Then, both tired of her adulation and wanting to make sure of it, I mocked and rejected her. A week later, I apologized, said let's be friends. She panted with happiness, and we started again.

For months, that's how it went—I rejected then reeled her back in, feeling my power to toy with her need. One day she finally looked me in the eye and said no. She would not be my friend. I felt stung, but I also felt strangely elated. For years, I couldn't figure out why. Now, perhaps, I can. Reenacting my parents' habitual drama, I'd taken on my father's role. Flatter, reject, apologize, lure the lover back. But this girl had at last refused to play. When I cheered for her walking away, maybe I was cheering for my mother, who, the next summer, would finally say, enough.

At Collegiate prep, which I'd loved with adolescent passion, I sat by the cinder track and thought of Vic, an athletic, blond eighteen-year-old running laps in turquoise sweats who would later become my boyfriend. I couldn't then have imagined that his brother Jack would die in a car crash just after graduation, leaving three brothers behind. Or that Vic, that beautiful boy, would die at fifty of a heart attack. Quite a phenomenon, those blond, pink-cheeked brothers. I wheeled past the Rounds Fine Arts Center, in whose library some of us had once been caged for detention. The obedient smart kids had committed some infraction that we'd thoroughly enjoyed.

I also dropped by our house on Bennett, where Bill Nichols now lived. He'd grown up across the street and never left the block. How could someone have been so still while I circled, it seemed, the globe? Entering my pale yellow house, I slipped into a parallel world of a life I hadn't led, where no one ever filled out change of address cards or packed so much as a spoon into a cardboard box. Bill had gone to Kelly Elementary a year behind Tara, Charla, and me. For my visit, he'd unearthed his yearbooks, so we sat at the kitchen table leafing through the half-sized pages. There we were, in inch-high black-and-white squares, Charla's blond hair in a white headband, her eyes framed by cat-eye glasses. The neighborhood back then had swarmed with kids. Five or six classes of fourth graders alone. I searched the page for Marty.

Marty was my fiancé. By which I mean he liked me, too. He'd been preceded in my affections by a kid I think was named Arnold, whom I dumped one day during recess. I was playing first base, praying that no one would throw me the ball. When Arnold hit a single and landed on first, I asked him who he wanted for president. Goldwater, he said. I could not like a boy who liked Goldwater. Before the next kid took his third swing, Arnold and I were through. Then came dark-eyed Marty, who rode bikes with me after school. We ran into a bigger wall than politics. Miss Bird caught us passing a note.

Miss Bird, as tiny as a titmouse and unmarried as a child, had been to Australia and lived with her sister. To me she seemed old. She kept her stuffed koala bear on a stool at the front of the classroom and talked to it as though it were real.

When Marty passed the note to me, which I had earlier passed to him, Miss Bird stormed up the aisle and snatched it. Technically, it wasn't a note; it was a marriage license. Written out in my best, loopy backhand cursive. The difference didn't matter to Miss Bird. Or rather, it did. She unfolded the paper and studied it. Her face flushed; she jammed the note into her pocket and, without looking at me, marched back to her desk.

After lunch she pulled me out of the recess line. "You, stay."

It wasn't the first time I'd been scolded by Miss Bird. She chastised me for writing backhand at least once a week, and for my untidy desk. But she'd never kept me in from recess.

I stood against the cinder block wall and watched the other children's feet shuffling outside to play. I thought she'd take me back into the classroom. Instead, Miss Bird led me down the hall to a little room by the principal's office, where she told me to sit down. I climbed into a tall chair on one side of a conference table, my feet dangling; she sat next to me at the end. I stared at the turquoise plaid of my favorite skirt. She exhumed the marriage license from her pocket, smoothed it out in front of me, and put her beaky face next to mine.

"This is very wrong," she said, slapping the note to underscore "very." I knew that passing notes was against the rules, but that's not what she meant. The very wrong thing was liking boys. I was too young. I could ruin my life. What was I thinking, getting a marriage license in the fourth grade? My face burned. I knew the marriage license was make-believe, but even that was wrong. She used up all of recess making sure I got the point.

How could a teacher who talked to a stuffed koala be so dense about children? I didn't know enough then to suspect something sexual, puritanical, behind her lashing out. Or to wonder if that's why she was Miss, not Mrs., Bird. Still, in my shame and confusion, I had a cloudy sense that her anger hid something bigger than Marty and me.

"Now, you need to talk to your mother about this," she said, winding things up. "Will you do that?"

I nodded, refusing to cry.

"Because if you don't, I will."

For three nights, the threat hung over me. Afraid of my mother, afraid of Miss Bird, I slept worse with every passing night. I would wake up early, at four or five, struggling to push myself back under the threshold of sleep. By the third night, I couldn't fall asleep at all. It felt like the middle of the night. I slid out of bed, slipped down the hall, and stood quietly in the doorway of my parents' lighted room. My mother sat on her bed with her back to the door, folding laundry. She shook out a towel and smoothed it on the bed with her hands.

"Mom?"

"Oh!" She jumped. She turned around. "You scared me."

Hot tears broke through the dam.

"Honey, what's wrong? Come here." She took me in her arms and stroked my head. Between sobs, the tale tumbled out.

"Oh, for Pete's sake," she said. It was my mother's worst swear. "That's ridiculous." I looked up at her face. She was angry. But not at me.

The day she went to straighten things out with Miss Bird, I decided I would not be proud; I wouldn't gloat that my mother had taken my side. I don't know what she said to Miss Bird, but my teacher never reprimanded me again, not even for writing backhand. The next time Marty came over to ride bikes, my mother washed and combed my hair for me and pinned my spit curls down with bobby pins. She told me to have a good time.

I'd been right about Miss Bird. There she was in the yearbook. Old. I didn't recognize which kid was Marty.

I learned to ride a bike in the backyard of that Bennett Street house. All day, secretly and without training wheels, I got up, fell off, got up, fell off, got up, stayed up, fell over, got up. By late afternoon, scraped from ankle to elbow, I could ride. Tara and I planned a circus for our parents; and after dinner at the appointed time, they exited the back door and took their seats. Tara's dolls did tricks on the swing set, including her clown doll Clancy with the plastic face, who swung by his knees from a cross bar. And then for the main attraction—I stood over the bike, pushed off, hoisted myself onto the pedals, and started pumping, wobbling, nearly crashing into the swing set but staying up, then, going faster, orbiting, orbiting the yard. My parents clapped and beamed.

It can't have surprised them. My mother would have been home that day checking on me from the kitchen window, tracking my progress, smiling to herself. When she arrived for the circus, she'd asked, her eyes twinkling, "And what are YOU going to do?" I grinned, nearly bursting, "YOU'll see." My father had also come to the circus prepared, though I didn't know it until I watched his home movies forty years later. There in grainy, moving color a circus performer with skinny legs and curly hair rides, pumping hard, standing upright on the pedals, so intent on her trick that she never noticed the camera.

Finally, after nearly thirty years away and more than a thousand miles, I reached house number thirteen. From my stakeout in the rented Toyota, I scanned the blank street. Magnolia, as quiet as I remembered it, is a modest, middle-class one-block street of mown lawns, attached garages, and low-slung ranch-style eaves. Some houses are postwar, and a few, like ours, are from the midsixties—bigger, with more brick, bigger yards, and double garages. But it's the same idea from one end of the block to the other. Each family in a privately owned, rectangular slice of American pie.

Unlike every other house in America, though, with its uniform blanket of fertilized turf, ours still sports a southwestern desert diorama. My parents' creation. Hillocks and yucca and broom grass and a wide curving swath of smooth round stones, each the size of a small cupped palm. The day the dump truck backed up to the curb and tipped its bed, two tons of river rock slid clattering through the truck's swinging gate into a great mound on the drive-way, dust clouds rolling into the air. We spent the afternoon lugging and dumping stones until we'd buried the black plastic that covered the newly built valleys and hills. I loved the muted grays and greens, the dusty reds and browns of the water-worn, sun-warmed stones. I think I loved them partly for the alliterative burble of "river rock," the sound of their former life in the shallow wash of a stream. In summer the sun heated them to scorching.

The entire effect is of a dry riverbed flowing out wide from under the house and narrowing to a stream near the curb. Along the verge of the river bank grows the plot of fescue I mowed every week until one day, before the dew had dried, I ran over the power cord and, not understanding why the motor had stopped, picked up the severed cable with my hand. Jolted to the soles of bare, wet feet, my synapses crackling, it took me a moment to realize I needed to let go.

The thing is, nobody else had a desert landscape, and nobody else planted fescue. "You gotta plant zoysia," the neighbors advised my parents. Zoysia's your hot weather grass, your winter grass. Durable. But zoysia gets planted in plugs, which makes new yards look like bare, dirt faces spotted with tufted moles. The plugs eventually spread and cover the dirt, but it takes years. Even then, you can still feel the plug humps under your feet. People used to being on the move don't necessarily have time to wait for zoysia, so my parents rented a red seed spreader, and in an hour, my father had planted a lawn. Days passed. The little seeds sat naked on the dirt. I worried, watching. I sat on the sidewalk and waited. Finally, about a week later, little blades started sprouting like a pale green haze, then grew more confident until a cool carpet unrolled across the yard.

Also unlike anyone else we knew, we had black woodwork and a sunken living room, exposed beams and an open stairwell to the basement with a wrought-iron rail. Among the muted shades of Kansas, we had shockingly colored walls. One bathroom in bright Crayola orange, the other primary blue. Hot yellow for Tara's room, chartreuse for Shannon's, electric pink for mine. In 1971, when I hit fourteen, I joined the counterculture by painting one wall electric orange.

I never considered the yard or decor as creative or bold, or even as a sign that my parents had intended to stay. Instead, I absorbed a sense of superiority and difference. The idea infused the yard, the architecture, the woodwork, the paint—we were better than our surroundings, better than the beige carpets and plastic hall runners of our neighbors. My parents had non-Kansas ideas about how to do things.

We were not really of this place.

The suburban house, vault of nuclear isolation, is the perfect place for secrets, the kind that damaged, deracinated families keep. Behind the closed door of our house—we rarely had company—we harbored not only unusual style, but rottenness at the seams of things. Beneath the placid surface of new floors and lacquered furniture lay the underground stream of betrayal, anxiety, and despair that I'd now followed through seven towns in two states. In Wichita it had churned in the night, threatening to rise and drown us; in daylight only a ripple fluttered now and then—what I recognize now as unspoken hurt, resentment, and unresolved conflict. My father's insatiable need, my mother's silent, self-wounding endurance.

Schooled in denial, I experienced the house—and remember it still—as tense, tidy, and quiet. My parents never fought in front of us. Sometimes, though, at an especially silent dinner, my mother's face would go dark, her chin start to quiver. She would swallow hard, clutch her napkin, and leave the table in tears. We'd hear her bedroom door close down the hall. Nobody asked and nobody said what was wrong.

I read my mother's wounded silence as a finger pointed at my father. To me she became blameless, he full of flaws. I searched for signs. His carpentry, for example, while ambitious and clever, frequently went askew. The drawer in my desk, which he'd built, hung aslant and wouldn't close; and the clever triangular picnic table with built-in benches was two inches too short. The cabinets in the garage fastened with hand-carved pegs that slipped into perfectly aligned eye-screw holes, but the doors hung from hinges at the top and lifted from the bottom. To retrieve a tennis racket or wrapping paper from a cabinet, we had to prop the door open on our heads.

He did make perfectly beautiful things, too. Intricate woven basket seats for curvilinear fifties chairs. Stylized, sculpted modernist heads. And mahogany and cherry chess sets, their rough shapes turned on a lathe and finished by hand, lined up on hand-parqueted boards. I relished the smell of sawdust, the humming lathe, the patient sanding of bishops and pawns, the symmetry of dark and light squares.

Behind the inventions of my father's clever hands, though, I always sensed some lack. By the time I reached fifth grade, his all-knowing facade had begun to crumble. To resolve a dispute with one of my sisters, I asked him, wasn't milk made of water? Yes, he said, yes it was; in fact, he added, all liquids contained a certain amount of water. I knew he was right about the milk, but his "in fact" addition sounded false and uncertain, a pretense of expertise. I felt the first stirrings of shame. But not more shame than he felt for himself.

When I was in my early thirties and teaching at Yale, my sisters and I flew to Wichita to celebrate my mother's retirement. In our old living room, which my mother had lent him for the occasion, we had our last collective encounter with my father. He stood by the window; I sat on the other side of the room, my arms crossed. Tara and Shannon sat on the couch. We all felt awkward, angry, hurt. He'd made little contact for years and for a while stood quietly in the heat of our attack. Then he blurted out that he felt intimidated by our accomplishments, especially my teaching at Yale.

In the seconds of silence that followed, a slice of light entered the room. He had never gone to college. Even his voracious reading had never erased the shame for what he did not have; it couldn't ease the sting of my PhD. I could see the pain and invitation in his eyes. Love me. Accept me.

It was a narcissist's ploy, shifting the focus from our hurt to his, asking for solace and attention. Still, years later, as I replayed the scene, I realized that until that moment, his feelings had never occurred to me. His complexity, fragility, insecurities, wounds had never counted. That day in Wichita, in too much pain from what his wounds had cost me, I let the moment pass. I never saw him again.

That was all inside, as Emily Dickinson says, where the meanings are. Outside was that yard.

As an adult with children of my own, driving through Arizona with the windows open to the desert heat, I finally understood my parents' diorama. They hadn't picked a landscape from a decorator's book. They had copied the land near Sedona that my mother loved, and the high desert of my father's boyhood westerns. The broom grass and yucca and river stones in that Wichita yard had stood for a place better than Kansas, a fantasy place that was also real, one they would get to eventually.

By the time my mother retired, she had clung to that yard as both map and destination for more than twenty-five years. When the time came, she sold everything connected with Kansas, even the little china bells we hung on the Christmas tree every year. When we heard about the bells, the three of us wept. "But all those things reminded me of so many terrible years," she said, stunned that we should care, surprised into seeing that our childhoods had also happened to us. "I hated Kansas," she said. "I didn't want to take it with me." Shedding Kansas like an old shoe, she headed west, where the desert she had planted on Magnolia grew on its own outside her Arizona window.

My father never made it out of Kansas or into the movies, though he landed a few small roles. He remarried twice and continued changing jobs, moving and moving again. He died at seventy, estranged and broke, in Topeka. Or was it Kansas City? For two weeks, nobody told us he was dead.

Parked on Magnolia, I suddenly knew that after two weeks' driving and all those miles, I didn't need to knock on the door.

When my father left and the rest of us stayed, I had just turned twelve. When I left for college at seventeen, my father's age when he shipped off into his reckless future, my mother's when she boarded the Northern Pacific for Yellowstone, I'd lived in the house for eight years. Long enough to be able to see, feel, hear, and smell every room without leaving the car.

I enter the house; hear my heels click on the neutral, checkered tiles of the entryway; listen to the hush of rust-colored shag in the perfectly dusted living room; smell the lemon oil my mother has rubbed into the ebony-stained woodwork with a soft, white cloth. Crossing the dining room to the glass patio doors, I look out to the dry backyard, where three family cats and a hamster lie in unmarked graves and an overgrown Christmas tree crowds the back fence.

Sliding the doors open, I step barefoot onto the hot cement to dry my hair in the sun. I peer through the basement windows, and on the wall, I see the wooden rack my father made for the Ping-Pong balls and paddles. And over there, the carpet samples he patch-worked together for our slumber parties and all-night games of triple solitaire. At the other end of the room sits his work bench, with nuts and bolts in baby-food jars hanging beneath a shelf.

Back inside, at the end of the hall, I enter my bedroom, close the door, and feel the dark cool of the days I slept through during the summers I worked the night shift at Denny's, always aware in my fit-ful sleep of the daylight and heat outside. And aware of my boyfriend camped out in the living room waiting for me to wake up. Or if my mother wasn't home, not waiting, but sliding in under the sheets and stroking my naked thigh until I woke enough to roll toward him, the afternoon a mingled dream of drowsy sex and sleep.

Out in the family room, I sit down at my piano. Every day for seven years, I settled into the molded plastic chair and, wrestling with the hard, slow action of the keys, worked through "The Sounds of Silence" or a Bach sonata or, later, Chopin. My mother, after wrangling first graders all day, peeled potatoes at the kitchen sink and patiently endured it.

In those fatherless years, my sisters and mother and I lived swathed in hush behind our separate bedroom doors. In summer the humming air conditioner amplified the stillness. In the dry air of winter, sparks crackled in the carpet when we walked the silent hall. My mother slipped into what nobody called depression; and one afternoon not too long after Dad left, Shannon, then nine, went downstairs to hang herself. She'd just flung her plastic jump rope over rafters when I came looking for her, which is all she really wanted. To be found, to be held, to be noticed. I pulled the rope down, and we rocked together in the living room for a while. Then I went back to my *Readers' Digest*, and she went back to her room. Tara took to sleeping on the floor when the disorder of her bedroom matched the chaos of her spirit and there was no other place empty enough to sleep. I played the piano. Music made me present. Gave me body, gave me voice. Which is why no matter what I played, I pounded it out as fast and fortissimo as possible.

This house inhabits me. It is the house I come to when I close my eyes, a house full of stories and lingering moods. On my first day home from college for the summer, for each of my first three years away, I wandered the rooms, touching beds, dressers, my mother's owl collection, my model lunar lander, taking the house back in. Touching ground.

Since then, I have lived in only one other place for as long as I did there. The Magnolia house has become for me, the child of nomads, a place that belongs to me. I didn't know that then. From the time I was ten, it was always the place I would leave behind.

We were expected to leave. Go off to college then go off for good. Most of my friends left long enough to earn a degree in education or dentistry or petroleum engineering, if their fathers worked in oil. Then they returned. For us success meant anyplace but Kansas. So I always assumed I would go. The first time I knew I really would, it was July, after my junior year of college. I stepped out of the air-conditioned house into the courtyard, the afternoon heat a blast that took my breath away. I was wearing my Denny's uniform of brown and orange polyester, support hose, and brown rubber-soled shoes. Before reaching the driveway, smothered in synthetics, I was drenched in sweat. There sat my butter yellow Ford Galaxy 500, sun glinting off the chrome. I'd just bought it, and it gave me wheels and it gave me style. But it also gave me a sense of my power to leave.

I opened the door with the hem of my skirt and lowered myself onto the dark red vinyl, pulling my too-short uniform under my thighs to keep from burning. Cranked open the windows, turned the key. Waited for the heat to turn to cool while the air conditioner blew. I cracked open the side window vent, pushed in the cigarette lighter, and waited for the click. The cool started to happen. I switched on the radio, turned up Santana. Turned it up again. The guitar bending those high, yearning notes, the Latin beat, hot thighs against vinyl, I turned it up again. It all felt like freedom. The hot air made for the exits, and I rolled the windows up. The lighter popped, I laid the hot coil against the tip of my Pall Mall, and inhaled, my head tilted back against the headrest. Acting in a movie of my wildness, I exchanged a cool glance with the girl in the mirror and exhaled a languid stream of smoke, tapping the ash outside. The music swelled, the cool air blew, I slipped the car into reverse. Dangled the cigarette just so, watched the smoke coil, checked my close-up in the mirror. I knew I was headed to Denny's for the night. But I also knew I was already more than gone.

Finishing my imaginary tour, I stand on the tiled landing and recall the day that my mother laid that little pile of laundry on the living room step. The moment that divided before from after.

I have mourned my father all of my life. I practiced that sentence for years, preparing for the day he would die. I thought his death wouldn't feel different from his absence. No different from being disowned, as we were, for the last seven years of his life. But now I wasn't so sure.

For years, nearly a lifetime, I had resisted the complexities of my father's life. Insisting on a simple, mythical story of an unfaithful, pain-inflicting man, I had exiled him from my heart, beyond the reach of my regard; it kept me safe from his dangerous and fleeting love. When I first imagined writing this book, I was determined to leave him out of it. But sitting in front of that house, I remembered that every time I'd moved in the last twenty years, I'd also carefully wrapped, padded, and taken with me Daddy Ball's sideboard.

Daddy Ball was my father's grandfather. The only steady, loving man in his life. Whenever Dad's parents separated or divorced (they married each other twice), my father and his mother found refuge at Daddy Ball's. There he found not only a substitute father but respite from his mother's overweening love. When he was young, Vivian made him her doll, keeping his then blond hair long and curly. When he was older and Vivian found herself single again and broke, she made him her little husband. The "man" who would love her, focus on her needs, and never leave her. In a black-and-white portrait of the two of them when my father was thirteen, he leans in close beside her, his lush hair swept back, his lips moist and full. He looks devoted; she, deserving of devotion. Entitled. Their airbrushed faces touch; her regal lips are tinted red. The photo used to give me the creeps. Now it just seems tragic.

At Daddy Ball's, my father also had his stepgrandmother Marian. Daddy Ball's second wife was only slightly older than Vivian and became the mother who loved my dad without conditions or demands. She let him be a boy. When the brothers lived together, she conducted them in amateur theatricals and played the organ. She taught my dad to sing "Tiny Bubbles."

In 1900, Daddy Ball built the sideboard. It stands waist high, with three cabinets for dishes along the bottom tier and three drawers on top, the center drawer deeper with its belly bowed out. An oval beveled mirror runs the length of the top, arms' width from end to end. And every inch of the piece is covered with images of California, which Daddy Ball burned into the wood and stained with dyes. Green leaves and red cherries twine around the mirror and the cabinet's top edge, and cherries tumble across the smaller drawers and down the curved legs. Red poppies with frowsy petals spill out of an oval frame on the big-bellied drawer and across the cabinet doors, their feathery green leaves blowing beside a rail fence.

The sideboard came to me when I was in my twenties, my grandmother's gift, at my father's suggestion. Someone's hot iron has left a pale, wedge-shaped burn on the top, and the mirror frame needs gluing. But it's held up through dozens of moves over the past hundred years. My daughters and I call it the Daddy Ball. And along with Vivian's Chinese silk shawl from San Francisco in the thirties, it's the most beautiful thing I own.

For years, I didn't know what to make of the gift. Why such an extravagant heirloom, when my father and I rarely spoke? Why did he think the sideboard should come to me, instead of to my sisters, especially to Tara, the oldest? And why did I feel so tenderly toward it?

I may never know what my father had in mind. I know I love the Daddy Ball for my great-grandfather's handwork, that union of labor and craft and care that still breathes the maker's presence. And the sideboard speaks so clearly of the place and time it was made, a California of orchards and wild poppies. It's rooted in place in a way I never have been. But like the Seeley family, it has also wandered. What came to life in Sacramento in my great-grandfather's workshop later moved around Los Angeles with my grandmother Vivian; spent years in Kansas in my mother's garage; went with me to New Haven, where the Seeleys first landed in the Americas; and when I moved to San Francisco, came home to the West Coast. For me it carries family and our migrations. It has covered a lot of ground.

But I think I have also treasured it as a way of loving my father.

Whenever I look at the Daddy Ball, I see the story of his childhood suffering and the times when he found ease. When he was genuinely, simply loved. The Daddy Ball reminds me that his acting ambitions grew not only from his father hunger but from Marian's living room theatricals, where he found acceptance and applause. And that his wood shop and chess sets were more than the dabbling of a hobbyist, but a reaching back to Daddy Ball and the work of his grandfather's hands. The sideboard takes me back to the man who was once a hurting boy, as I was his hurting daughter. It tells me that although he inflicted pain, he suffered it, too. When he gave me the Daddy Ball, here, he said, is safety. Here is pain and healing. This is also who I am.

In giving me this gift, perhaps my father knew that I—the writer like him, the handcrafter like him, the family beauty like him, the aloof one most determinedly distant from him—would be the one most likely to read the runes on the Daddy Ball and let him emerge from the pages of a different story. And maybe I knew that going back to Kansas would one day help me find it.

Before. And after. Standing on the threshold of that house, his death did feel different from his absence. Different from being disowned. For the first time, I thought not only of his leaving but also of his grief. Of what happened on the other side of that door the day he strode down the walk and drove away. Of what he left behind—his workshop, tools and benches, his paintings and chairs, my desk, the picnic table, and the cabinets he'd built in the house that his brief success had made. His daughters. And of what he lost later when he shut us out completely, the women who could not be managed and would not be charmed.

Clinging to hurt is like holding your breath. It deprives the heart of oxygen. If the last few months had taught me anything, it was the importance of breathing. Breathe in, things happen, breathe out, they're over, first they hurt, then they slip away into the flux of time. In breathing out, letting go, the heart opens. The ego stops demanding an apology. It allows the other, the perpetrator, to appear in his wholeness and hurt. What was left but forgiveness?

We all left Magnolia Street, one by one. Mom was the last to go.

Her presence suddenly filled the house. I saw her coming down the front walk in her pedal pushers and Keds, crossing the river of stones, kneeling in the grass with her gardening prong, and digging out a dandelion. There she was, shoveling snow, scraping ice from the windshield while her car warmed up in the driveway. I saw her going and coming, trimming trees, mowing the lawn, carrying in groceries, scrubbing floors, typing letters on her clackety black Royal, paying bills, grading papers, crying in her room. She may have been broke, afraid, depressed, overwhelmed, alone. But she held up that roof like a Hercules, and she never folded.

When she moved away, none of us saw her go. But I could imagine. Organizing her garage sale, shedding her Kansas past, packing what little she wanted to keep in neatly labeled boxes. Among the things she'd never jettisoned in forty years of moving were her photos of Aspen, the place of her first great western adventure. In a few days, she'd be in Arizona, settling in among mountain views, amid her desert garden.

I envisioned her on her last day in Wichita, walking one more time through empty, echoing rooms, then closing the door behind her. Taking a backward glance at the same view I had now. A yard full of fescue and river rock. Charla's house and mine.

I shifted in my seat. In the front yard, the fluffy-seeded tufts at the tips of the broom grass had grown higher than the eaves of the house.

PART TWO

···

Widening the Circle

There is the place that happens, and
the place that happens to you.

EAVAN BOLAND
"The Woman, the Place, the Poet"

....

CHAPTER SIX

Kansas Becomes Me

At the end of my two weeks on the road, I had fallen in love with Kansas. Or let myself admit I'd loved it all along. Every spring for the next five years, I got the itch. Kansas. I still feel the pull, not of nostalgia, but of long horizons and open sky, tall grass and wheat fields, of wind and the smell of ozone before a summer storm.

I would follow its lure for the next four summers, and cancer held itself in abeyance. At least once a day, I remembered with a start—cancer—and knew it might return. But I usually remembered to breathe, acknowledge my fear—there you are—and breathe out, letting it go. Most of the time, cancer seemed less of a threat and more of a companionate reminder. Like a light that casts an enlivening glow on everything it touches.

Back in San Francisco my hamster hair started looking human, my energy gradually returned, and in an unprecedented act of daring—at least for me—I browsed the personals on Salon.com and met a new man. His online profile said he was tall, a filmmaker, a Buddhist. In answer to the question, "Why would a woman want to know you?" he'd written, "I've done a lot of work on myself. I don't need a woman for caretaking." A grown-up, it sounded like, a man most unlike my father. Most unlike P.

On our first date, we navigated the new thin ice of acquaintance and possibility. Over salads at Café Flor, I recounted my recent trip to Kansas; he'd grown up in Illinois. Over tea, we talked about death. I mentioned my news—cancer—and watched it flow through him like water. Frederick's gaze was steady, unguarded, unalarmed. It reminded me of my meditation teacher on the night of my first class. When I explained why I'd come—I'd just been diagnosed with cancer and hoped that meditation would help during treatment— Sakti Rose looked at me without flinching, taking it in like a breath that arises and goes.

Frederick said he's diabetic, insulin dependent, so he thinks about death. But he talked easily of his own mortality, not the way most people do. "Of course," they say, when they hear I've had cancer, "we could all be hit by a bus tomorrow." They believe in the idea of the bus but don't really believe in the bus. It's an abstraction, a truism, not something real. But Frederick spoke as though he believed it and lived as though it were true. It made sense, of course. Frederick meditates. He breathes. He knows how to dwell, not in fear of an unknown future, but deeply in the life that is. We'd moved from small talk to hallelujah in less than an hour.

Over the months that followed, while we learned each other's stories, I also kept a steady eye on Kansas. There was still something there I needed to learn, though I didn't yet know what. I knew that I felt drawn to the stories that lay on the landscape, bigger stories than those of my own small life.

Take this one, for example: Goodland, where I'd lost and found my kindergarten, began in the middle of a boneyard. In the center of the Great Plains, across a swath from Canada to the Texas panhandle, 50 million buffalo were slaughtered in less than twenty years. When I think of that, the scene comes flooding in. First, the tumult of stampeding hooves, rifle fire flashing from Rock Island train windows or horseback, one buffalo, another, halting in its thunderous run and sinking down. Then, the more-focused sounds of purposeful work, steel against sinew and hammer against steel, men slicing a red furrow around each animal's neck, down its belly, pounding a long metal spike through its nose, staking it to the ground. A hook through the neck, a crack of the whip, the strain of a horse, the buffalo coat ripped whole from flesh that is still warm.

Eastern consumers want only the hides, so the hunters leave the carcasses to rot in the sun. After the men ride away, death has its moment of stillness. Then comes the syncopated buzz of black flies laying eggs in the meat. In the afternoon, turkey vultures, clumsy and squawking, squabble over their prize. Coyotes in the evening, skulking and snuffling, tear into death with their teeth. Maggots and time dissolve away the rest. In the end, there is only the silence of bones. Thick enough in western Kansas to turn the ground white. And to lure a man named Joseph Collier away from wherever he'd come. He built himself a little sod house and took up work as a bone collector for the fertilizer trade while waiting for his crops to thrive. After eight years alone, he heard rumors of the railroad coming through. Before he probably had time to contemplate, a hundred new neighbors had arrived in the new boomtown of Goodland.

Or there's this story: In the summer of 1870, the season of buffalo hunts and ripening maize, the Osage nation lost its tribal lands. Since 1825 their reserve—millions of acres protected by treaty—had stretched nearly halfway across present-day Kansas, from the eastern edge at the Missouri line to the Arkansas Forks, where the Big and Little Arkansas rivers meet. Through this point runs the ninety-eighth meridian, a line that divides the continent—tallgrass prairies to the east, short-grass plains to the west, a swath of mixed grass in the middle. After white settlement, farming east of the line—where rain usually falls—became a pretty sure bet. That's why, in a wet summer, the big bluestem grass might grow higher than a tall man's head. Farming much west of the line was for fools. Or for folks willing to empty the Ogallala aquifer and leave the place hard and dry as a summer stone. Since the 1930s, people have been more than willing. As I recently overheard a farmer say, "That water, she's nearly gone." Left to its true nature, western Kansas, home to Goodland and Hays, is sagebrush and yucca country, not given to industry that requires much rain.

Native tribes understood these regions. They had lived along the Arkansas Forks, that fulcrum between east and west, for eleven thousand years. Over time the valley that they called the "Ute-cha-og-gra" became a hub where sedentary farming tribes to the east and plains nomads to the west met for trade. Networks spread so wide that tribes along the Arkansas Forks stored corn in pots made by Pueblo Indians in the desert Southwest.

Eleven thousand years is a long time. Over the millennia, different peoples occupied the area, and each stayed for generations. Roots ran deep. Like their predecessors in the region, the Osage, who had migrated to the Ute-cha-og-gra sometime before the seventeenth century, made no distinction between themselves and the place they lived. Some oral traditions related that they had been sent to earth by the wellspring of spirits, the god Wacondah. Others told of the god of rain and the Great Buffalo Bull who protected their crops. Collectively, they called themselves the Children of the Middle Waters. In summers, they fished the Little Arkansas, the "Elcah," growing squash, corn, and beans in plots beside the river. Like their Kansa relatives and the Pawnee, they hunted bison twice each year.

Then in 1863, the same year he freed the slaves, President Lincoln, with Congressional approval, began extinguishing all Indian land titles in Kansas. By 1867 the Shawnee, Seneca, Wyandot, Ottawa, and Confederated Peoria tribes had all ceded their lands; the Sauk and Fox had been dispelled. The Osage held on to their lands longer than most. But in late September 1870 they were ordered to Indian Territory, soon to be called Oklahoma.

As the people prepared to go, the *Wichita Vidette* reported that "the air was filled with the cries of the old people, especially the women, who lamented over the graves of their children, which they were about to leave for ever."

Given a choice, the Osage would not have left their buried children behind. Those graves tied them to the place as much as did the fishing waters of the Little Arkansas and the pantheon of their gods. Days after the tribe led their ponies south, workers' shovels began demolishing graves all over the Ute-cha-og-ogra. Some newcomers sent Native remains to the Smithsonian; others brutalized the relics.

The local paper reported that at one building site, "several boys bore away the skulls, banner-like, swinging them by the eyeless sockets on the ends of two cottonwood poles."

A hundred years later and a mile from the Arkansas Forks, where the Osage had lived and buried their dead, my parents planted their fescue and broom grass and laid down a river of stones. Like most Americans, they could hardly have imagined the Osage sense of place, of belonging in a tight web of nature, identity, and belief. But they knew what attachment could mean. They, too, had left a child's grave behind.

I know it grieved them. Once, on vacation out of state, we visited the baby's grave. It lay under a small brass plaque hidden in the grass, one in a long row of identical markers. When my father finally found it, he crouched over the grave, pressed his fingers to his eyes, and sobbed. Riveted by the sight of him crying, I hardly noticed my mother. I felt excluded by their grief, unsteadied by knowing that this other child had been theirs, too.

Remembering my parents' sorrow over a buried child, more than anything else, has lifted the Osage from history into the living world for me, taught me to hear their keening. And knowing the Osage story has given Wichita and the house on Magnolia a role in a longer, and sadder, story, a story larger than the span of my childhood or the scope of my own family's life.

Gathering other stories, I've haunted abolitionist graveyards and churches near Manhattan (the Little Apple) and visited the remarkable Brown v. Board of Education Museum in Topeka. There, in Linda Brown's former elementary school, I bent to sip from a child-sized water fountain and felt how small those children were. Children who, by standing for a cause, learned to stand in the fire.

I've rambled through Riverside Park in Independence in the southeastern corner of the state, on the verge of the Verdigris River. Playwright William Inge grew up just blocks away in a large, two-story white frame house with a wraparound porch and a genteel facade.

When I stood in his backyard next to the clothesline pole and peered across the alley to the neighbors', and later when I strolled past the picnic benches in the park, past the boat launch and bandstand and zoo, I imagined how *Picnic* and *Come Back, Little Sheba* had come to Inge's mind, how the struggle between classes and between midwestern propriety and the dark urgings of sex had unfolded in his neighborhood. Or how the family tragedy of *The Dark at the Top of the Stairs* had sprung from inside his boyhood home.

Inge's Kansas differs in its particularities from the world I knew, but its tangle of sex, morality, and masculine dysfunction seems chillingly familiar. I see my father in the men ill-equipped to obey the dictates of class or culture. Men who feel emasculated by a changing world or who hide their feelings of worthlessness by seducing women other than their wives. I see my mother in the women who endure abuse or the return of profligate husbands. And in every character who hears the lure of elsewhere every time a train whistle blows, I see my younger self.

I've driven out east of Independence through the coal-mining country of the Kansas Ozarks, where hills shorten the views, trees thicken, and myriad creeks run through. After crossing Coal Valley Road late one afternoon, I passed through the tiny village of West Mineral. Strip-mining had flattened much of the hilly terrain. Standing beside one gaping crater that had since filled with water, I gazed up into the now defunct innards of Big Brutus, the 1850-B Bucyrus-Erie electric shovel. A machine sixteen stories high, 11 million pounds, Big Brutus gobbled ninety cubic yards in every shovelful, scraping the soil from atop the veins of coal, twenty-four hours a day for eleven years. The day I stopped to see it was a cloudless 104 degrees; I couldn't stand being outside for more than a few minutes. I thought of the miners, who, even in that heat, would have kept working around the clock. I thought of the families who settled that corner of Kansas—Italian, Slav, Welsh, and Irish—and forged a solidarity so strong that they, including the workers' wives, frequently shut down the mines. In a photo in the Big Brutus museum, the workers seem on the verge of disappearing into the hill of stones behind them, each stone the size and shape of a human head.

I've driven south to the Red Hills near Oklahoma and west to the desolate, fossil-rich Chalk Bluffs. In central Kansas I've traveled through the Cheyenne Bottoms Wetlands, where red-winged blackbirds stand sentry atop the waving tips of cattails. I've driven through Paradise and Plainville and Emporia, where famed journalist William Allen White crowed about Kansas from his office at the *Emporia Gazette*. I know where Waldo is and how to contra dance, which I learned at the Prairie Festival in Salina. At the Konza Prairie preserve near Manhattan, I've watched buffalo atop the hills catching the afternoon breeze, the summer's new babies nudging their mothers' bellies.

And I've been to Nicodemus, twice. Settled by ex-slaves who fled the South after Reconstruction, Nicodemus lies just north of the Solomon River, where the Smoky Hills meet the High Plains. Still an all-black town, it bloomed as frontier towns tended to—growing from dugouts into a scattering of sod houses, then into wood-frame stores and churches on Main Street, a village surrounded by farms. But when the railroads bypassed Nicodemus, the town began to fail. It's been dwindling every since.

The first time, I went through at evening, when the streets were still. The fifty or so residents had gone indoors for the night. A TV flickered blue inside an apartment at the Nicodemus Arms. Most of the houses were gone, the lots empty. In a grassy, vacant yard, a rusty pump handle stood, waiting. Tumbleweeds had pushed up through the asphalt.

The second time, I went for Nicodemus's annual Homecoming Festival, when former residents and settlers' descendants return. On a bench under a shade tree near the 1885 African Methodist Episcopal church, I sat with Don Moore, who'd lived in Nicodemus his whole life. His dark, lined face was shaded by his straw cowboy hat, and he seemed puzzled by my interest in the town. For a while he was reticent, like plains people tend to be, answering my questions about how many people lived there and how long he had farmed before retiring. But after a while he kept talking. He was afraid that his wife, like some other folks he knew, had "old-timer's disease." Sometimes it seemed like she didn't recognize him. When he'd come into the room that morning, she'd acted like he wasn't there. Finally, staring at nothing, she'd asked, "Did you bring my clothes?" He had no idea what she meant.

Another friend of his, also beset by "old-timers'," had been in the nursing home, and Don had gone to visit. The man hadn't been eating, but when Don arrived, his friend recognized him right away. Don said, "I think you'd better eat your dinner," and the friend replied, "I believe I will." When he finished his meal, Don asked him what kind of ice cream he wanted, chocolate or vanilla. He took chocolate. When Don left, the friend said, "Don, you'd better come back to see me," and Don promised that he would. A week later, the man died.

Don shook his head and looked at the ground. People were arriving in rental cars and suvs, pulling up in front of the meeting hall, while, behind us, white workers finished erecting the stage in the park. Don said that when he was a child, he knew some old people in Nicodemus who'd been slaves.

Once the jazz band started up, I bought Don a beer, and he seemed a little unsure about whether his pride was hurt. He said he'd never had a woman buy him a drink. I said it was all I could do to repay him for his stories. So he seemed to take it as a fair trade.

Little by little, with every conversation, every museum, every mile, I take Kansas more deeply into myself. Driving the long straight roads or the hilly crooked ones, I settle into the comfort of knowing and belonging, slowly losing my fear of the plains' empty reaches and relishing the different textures of the wind. I have finally shucked my stereotypes and city condescension, the snobbishness of a lucky escapee, and can appreciate the people I meet, not dismiss them for what they think or wear or know about the world. They have a rooted experience I envy.

One late July, I left Lawrence about seven in the morning after a great, cracking thunderstorm the night before. It was a cool seventy-five, the sky a soft gray, the rain-brightened trees still dripping. I stopped for breakfast near Lecompton at a picnic shelter beside the road. I've come to love this about Kansas—the picnic shelters that appear on quiet roads in the middle of what might seem like nowhere. Signs with a picnic table icon announce their approach. Picnic Table 1 Mile, 500 Yards, Next Turn. They're often set under shade trees or under a canopy built for shade, and I sometimes stop out of gratitude for that simple gesture of kindness and the pleasure of country quiet.

I settled onto the picnic bench and poured a bowl of muesli and soymilk. I still travel with rarified food. Tiny grasshoppers were popping in the damp grass, a bumblebee dipping into clover. Crickets fiddled somewhere in the weeds. A man in a starched blue shirt and khakis had parked his car at one end of the circular drive and was walking from one end to the other, arms folded, head bent. When he reached the far end, he turned and started back. I wondered whether he might be praying or walking off sadness or maybe an argument at home. We gave each other space for speculation.

That day, I'd be driving west across the state, reaching Goodland by nightfall. I'd eat dinner at China Garden and spend one more night in Kansas before Denver and the airplane home. By now I knew the changing landscapes along the route. From east to west, I would traverse the glacier fields of the northeast that give that corner its New England hills and trees, then the sensuous rise and swoop of the Flint Hills, tallgrass pastures, mixed grass prairie, short grass plains, and nearing the western edge, the flat pan of sea-fossil rangeland and red turkey wheat. I could predict with near certainty that the rain clouds would vanish about the time I reached Salina and that yucca would appear before I passed through Hays. I would see grasslands and tree-lined creeks, hedgerows of Osage orange, irrigation sprinklers in cornfields, the pale stubble of freshly cut wheat. I knew that by late October the shorn fields would be wearing the daring chartreuse of winter wheat, a shock of color in the otherwise tawny palette of winter.

It was too late for wild strawberries, too early for asters, just right for the purple wildflowers of summer—self-heal, prairie clover, blazing star. At the verge of the roads, native grasses would be heavy with seed—Indian grass, switchgrass, big and little bluestem, prairie dropseed, slough and wild rye, and porcupine grass with its long, raspy quills.

I knew that my picnic table sat at the center of Bleeding Kansas. John Brown country. Antislavery warrior Old John Brown with his flinty eyes, stern brow, and tight, straight mouth. In an early daguerreotype, he poses with his arms crossed, thick dark hair swept back from his forehead. In later images, he wears a snow-white Old Testament prophet's beard, his thick white hair rising up like the dead at Judgment Day. He seems made of adamant.

"Sometimes," Stephen Vincent Benét wrote in his Civil War epic, *John Brown's Body*, "there comes a crack in Time itself," when a great force, "call it the mores, call it God or Fate," moves to change a thing

> that has stood so long
It seems implanted as the polar star.

. . . .

> And when [that force] moves,
It will employ a hard and actual stone
To batter into bits an actual wall
And change the actual scheme of things.
> John Brown
Was such a stone.

Born in 1800, John Brown came to the new Kansas territory at fifty-five, armed with a well-thumbed King James Bible and a militant hatred of slavery. He also brought his army of five sons and enough firearms to practice what he preached. In doing so, Brown followed legions of abolitionists who had been summoned by conscience to Kansas. Since the federal government, eager to wash its hands of the matter, had decided that Kansans themselves would vote whether to enter the union as Free State or slave, immigrants had been pouring in. Skirmishes between abolitionist and proslavery settlers became routine—as did gun battles between opposing militia groups, and guerilla incursions into settlements on both sides of the question and both sides of the Kansas–Missouri border.

In October 1855 Brown arrived in the Free State town of Osawatomie, twenty miles west of Missouri. There he helped build cabins for his sons and for his half sister Florella and her husband Samuel Adair, who had also come to Kansas as Free Staters. His wife Mary stayed behind in North Elba, New York, a black farming settlement in the Adirondacks, where the Browns had lived for seven years supporting the settlers and living among their neighbors as social and political equals. It was an ideal to which Brown had committed his life, and he had intended to stay. But then Kansas called to him as even North Elba had not and as nothing else would until Harpers Ferry.

Within weeks of entering the territory, Brown and his sons were guarding polling places in the territorial election, protecting ballot boxes from proslavery Missourians who flooded the precincts to vote. Two months later, he marched with twenty men overnight from Osawatomie to Lawrence, thirty-five miles as the crow flies, to head off Missourians bent on destroying the city. When the governor brokered an agreement, war was averted; but as captain of the Liberty Guards, Brown had assumed his first military command.

A guerilla fighter who took on pseudonyms like Nelson Hawkins and Shubel Morgan as he slipped in and out of the state, Brown operated in the shadows. He kept his camp in the woods along the Middle Ottawa Creek, with horses saddled and ready, and saw himself in biblical terms. He wrote in a letter that he and his men were "hiding from our enemies like David of old finding our dwelling with the serpents of the rock, and wild beasts of the wilderness." And like David, he and his men routinely defeated the Goliath of more-numerous proslavery foes.

In the late summer of 1856, however, the press began alluding to other legends. The *Kansas City Enterprise* reported that "this Brown . . . is fast taking rank with guerrilla chiefs of Mexico, and the robber bands of Cane Hill, Arkansas." Brown's notoriety sprang from a series of exploits that had begun the previous May.

Near midnight on May 24, Brown, four of his sons, and two other men had entered proslavery cabins; pulled five men from their beds; and on the banks of Potawatomie Creek, hacked them to death with swords. Brown called the killings justice for the recent burning of Lawrence and the murders of five Free Staters. Just or no, this single act of retribution launched the bloodiest year in Kansas's undeclared civil war.

On June 2, two weeks after Potawatomie, Brown and company, greatly outnumbered, defeated proslavery forces at the Battle of Black Jack south of Lawrence and took twenty-five fighters prisoner. After three days, they released their captives and dismantled the Ottawa Creek encampment as though it had never been. Brown was then on the move—to Lawrence; then to Topeka to meet with an illegal Free State legislature; on to Nebraska City, where he linked up with a Free State military caravan; and finally into Missouri. On August 28 he returned to Osawatomie in high spirits, driving 150 Missouri cattle into town. It was only right, he believed, to seize the property of those who had gained it on the backs of slaves.

To this point, Brown had operated with impunity. He seemed untouchable. But two days later, the war came to Osawatomie. Two-hundred-fifty proslavery troops led by General John W. Reid arrived to put an end to John Brown. They faced off at the Marais des Cygnes River, which meets Potawatomie Creek a quarter mile out of town. Along the banks, thick with brush and trees, Brown ran behind his line of men, urging them on, shouting to "fire low." The firefight was immense, the air so loud with gunfire and cannon that his men could not hear him. Brown's son Frederick died first. The rest of Brown's forces soon had to give way and began falling back through the brush. Some dove into the river and were shot dead as they swam. Brown and a few other men fled farther down the bank and waded across, bullets searing the water around them.

When he finally reached high ground, defeat certain, John Brown stood beside his son Jason and watched Osawatomie burn. "God sees it," he is reported to have said. "I have only a short time to live—only one death to die, and I will die fighting for this cause. There will be no peace in this land until slavery is done for." Having anointed himself an instrument of destiny, Brown began preparing for Harpers Ferry.

Brown's carelessly planned raid on a federal arsenal in a Southern state, flanked by only twenty-one men, Harpers Ferry seemed a greater failure of judgment than even the killings at Potawatomie Creek. Brown's hoped-for reinforcements, though organized and ready, were not told that he had decided to move early. And the Southern slaves he had hoped to free did not rise up to join him. It was, on all counts, a disaster.

Yet when Brown was hanged for treason in Charlestown, Virginia, on December 2, 1859, as an example to anyone who dared challenge the sovereignty of Virginia, abolition had the martyr it needed. Throughout the Free States, millions gathered at prayer meetings and rallies to mourn Brown's death and recommit themselves to the battle. Understandably, the slaves of Virginia held no public displays of feeling. Still, more than one barn in the area around Charlestown went up in arsonists' flames.

John Brown could have died at any point in Kansas—at Potawatomie, Black Jack, Lawrence, Osawatomie. He could have been killed rustling cattle or escorting slaves to freedom, and he would have been remembered as one among many who fought to make Kansas free. But Harpers Ferry guaranteed his apotheosis. It made his life a coherent whole, honed the rough edges, diminished the flaws, excused Potawatomie, and made all the decisions and turns in the road seem directed toward one glorious end. It made the man a shining myth. By its light, the man who had failed as a wool merchant and impoverished his family would be compared to Nat

Turner, to Leonidas, to Christ. Harriet Tubman, whom he called his "General," considered Brown, not Abraham Lincoln, the "liberator of her race." Emerson wrote that John Brown, "if he shall suffer, will make the gallows glorious like the cross."

In dying for abolition, Brown also lit the fuse of coming war. William Lloyd Garrison, famed editor of the *Liberator*, evoked the language of dime westerns: "In firing his gun, John Brown has merely told what time of day it is. It is high noon. Thank God." Longfellow turned to the Old Testament but foretold the same future. On the day Brown hanged, Longfellow wrote in a letter, "This is sowing the wind to reap the whirlwind, which will come soon."

In press reports and books, images of fire, sparks, and heavenly light fell like Roman candles over Brown's last days. For all his failures, Benét wrote, Brown "knew how to die," and had

> six weeks to burn that hoarded knowledge
> In one swift fire whose sparks fell like live coals
> On every State in the Union.

Thoreau wrote in "The Last Days of John Brown" that "John Brown's career for the last six weeks of his life was meteor-like, flashing through the darkness in which we live. I know of nothing so miraculous in our history."

Knowing he had the national ear, for Old John Brown made good press, he wrote his jeremiad in prison. His nearly one hundred letters, many of which found their way into print, denounced slavery and prescribed war. He even handed his executioner a note, a message he surely knew would make the national papers: "I John Brown am now quite certain that the crimes of this guilty land will never be purged away but with Blood."

The North, Benét wrote, "hung fables" about his final hours. He had become the Atonement, the "crucified Christ."

The light of martyrdom casts no shadows. It's hard to find the man beneath the myth. For a start, though, I love this eyewitness account of Brown retreating across the Marais des Cygnes the day Osawatomie burned. George Grant recalled that Brown looked a "queer figure, in a broad straw hat and a white linen duster, his old coattails floating outspread upon the water and a revolver held high in each hand, over his head." This makes Brown a physical man to me in a moment of real time, a man with water in his boots and floating coattails, an odd straw hat and linen duster, adrenaline pumping and the presence of mind amid the noise and smoke of guns to keep his pistols dry. And to hold the death of his son Frederick in a small, tight place in his mind—a hard nugget he would, when things got quiet and he had time, turn over in his hand to feel its weight.

Just the day before, I'd been to the Brown-Adair cabin in Osawatomie. In the hewn-log walls, the marks from John Brown's ax seemed as fresh as the day he'd made them. Ducking under low doors, barely clearing the ceiling beams, I tried to imagine the prophet with his madman's beard and avenging fury in those small rooms. A Jesus, a David, a saint. But the cabin made him ordinary, both smaller and more human than the legend. A man who built the house in the cold after finding his sons, who had arrived in Kansas ahead of him, shivering in their tents. A man who ate from his sister Florella's blue china plates and drank tea from her blue china teapot. A man tender enough to give his daughter Ruth the small reed organ with narrow, iron pedals and scrollwork legs that sits in the cabin's parlor.

On the July afternoon that I visited, I stood on the footbridge near the Adair cabin and peered toward the bend where Potawatomie Creek meets the Marais des Cygnes, the site of so much death. A sluggish, muddy stream flowed below me, and I listened for the dying cries of five men in the night as Brown's men raised their swords and then the silence. I imagined gunpowder exploding and the bedlam of men firing from the underbrush or dying in the water the day John Brown uttered his fateful words. I could see smoke from the fires, the flames reflected in his wrathful, future-seeing eyes. That smoke merged with smoke from the cooking fires of Potawatomie Indians who had camped along the river in the ages before John Brown. The shadow of a high cloud raced across the water.

Time to pack up the muesli and head west. I had a day filled with Kansas ahead of me. And a head full of Kansas to fill up my days.

Back in California with my new collection of Kansas travel tales, Frederick asked, a bit puzzled, "Why do you love Kansas?"

There is always some mystery in the reasons for love. But there is also this.

Back on the first night of my meditation class, during those first weeks of cancer treatment and what I've come to call "the troubles," we had finished tasting the raisin and lay on our backs in the darkened room. We closed our eyes, each quiet in our own separate space on the floor, and practiced a body scan.

"Bring your attention to the top of your skull." The top of my head began to tingle. "Now move your attention down the back of your head." As though some inner eye or hand swept over each part in turn, I felt my forehead, eye sockets, cheeks, and chin. Each came awake under the touch of attention, then receded from notice as I released it and moved on, to shoulders, arms, elbows.

"Your mind will wander; that's natural. When it does, simply note it, let it go, and bring your attention back to your body. Focus, concentrate." I focused, and thoughts intruded—cancer, P, his new love, my grief—but instead of clinging to them, I labeled those stories "Thinking" and sent them drifting away like feathers on the tide. As each wave receded, something in me began to loosen, and the tight band of sadness and fear that had held me for weeks began to slip its knot from around my throat.

We noticed each finger, knee, ankle, then let go and moved on. Letting go, I thought, is the point. Pay attention, focus, let go. Soft snoring arose from somewhere across the room. When we finished with our toes, we lay still, arms at our sides, palms softly open, and we breathed, giving attention now to our whole body. Mine floated, every part calm and alive. For whole seconds at a time, I felt free of P and cancer and my coming surgery and leaving the Victorian house. Three taps of a bell brought our attention back to the room, the sound of the traffic outside, the lights from the streetlamps. We sat up and looked around, calm, rested, slowed.

Before meditating we had been shy of each other, strangers wrapped in protective silence, skittish glances, and downcast eyes. But now eyes made contact. The blond woman with whiplash and I looked at one another and didn't look away. I looked at the young man whose anxiety wouldn't let him sleep, and he looked back at me, both of us in that moment unguarded and unafraid.

Fear so often gets in the way of deep connection, breeding as it does defensiveness and distance. I will probably always fear abandonment, deep-rooted as it is in a childhood of moving and my father's many partings. But these new skills in paying attention and letting go now help me to recognize my fear whenever it arises and to let it float away. And in that moment of profound vulnerability, to not look away.

So when I came home that second summer after another Kansas journey and Frederick asked, "Why do you love Kansas?" all I could think to answer was, "Why do I love you?" That doesn't answer the mystery of attraction. But the ability to look at the other and not look away, to notice, acknowledge, and let go of fear, or of grief or the past, is the foundation of intimacy. It makes loving a place, as well as a person, possible.

One month after that second trip to Kansas, almost a year since our lunch at Café Flor, Frederick and I stood before an altar in the garden of the Green Gulch Zen Center. We bowed to one another, lit candles, looked at each other unflinchingly, and then we said our vows. A tall bouquet of sunflowers stood at our feet.

....

CHAPTER SEVEN

Sacred Bundles, Secret Maps

During that second summer, at the time of ripening wild plums, I stopped at a high, lonely place above the banks of the Republican River, the site of a Kitkehahki village. The inhabitants had left in the early 1820s, and now the only signs of their presence were a few artifacts and the round depressions in the earth where they'd built their lodges. I walked through the village reading placards that detailed what excavators had found. In one lodge, a ceremonial altar and a sacred bison skull. In another, a woven grass mat, paints, and piles of shelled corn. A pottery figurine. Two stone hoes, a kettle. A cache of corn inside a storage pit. Now the archaeologists had moved on, too; dry summer grass covered the lodge floors. Someone was keeping it mowed.

From the edge of the village, I looked out toward the bluffs beyond where the horses had grazed, to where the Kitkehahki had buried their dead. And except for a wheat field that clambered up one side of the hill and a tree here and there, I saw the same view the Kitkehahki had when they'd last lived there. For twenty miles in every direction, wind-rippled tall grass blanketed the earth, gold, russet, and tan. The people could have seen their enemies—mostly Kaw and Osage in those times—approaching for nearly a day.

But from atop that place, they also saw, as I did, a world made mostly of sky. It was powerfully, achingly present. A blue turned fierce and blanched with light, the sun riding high in its summer arc like an all-seeing, unblinking god.

That sky made it easy to believe that in the beginning, the god Tirawahat (Vault of the Heavens) created the stars and that these star gods, in turn, created humans in their own image. And easy to understand why the Pawnees had created their earth lodges, round and domed, to map their beliefs and mirror the shape of the heavens. Each entryway faced east, the direction of the Morning Star, god of fire and war. On the west side stood the altar—presided over by Evening Star, goddess of light and fertility—and a sacred buffalo skull.

The museum, built over an excavated lodge floor, was also round and domed, its entryway facing east. Inside, it was cool and dimly lit, cathedral-like and hushed. Hollow voices from across the room wavered and dissipated. In the center lay a hearth, charred from cooking fires and encircled by post holes. Fallen beams lay on the tamped earth. The remains of an altar stood at the western edge.

A world can spring from a fragment. The paradox of ruins. Walls of sod blocks rose from the hard floor; a roof stretched across, made of saplings and thatch; and the lodge filled with a Kitkehahki family, forty or fifty extended kin. Some sewing moccasins, others making arrows, one lighting a fire, one stirring a pot, old women caring for children. At night, everyone sleeping on platforms under the eaves.

A medicine bundle hung over the altar space, taking me further into that world. Deep inside its leather wrappings and the memories of generations lay the story of a vision from the gods. Its other contents had governed the family's sacred ritual: A pipe with a stone bowl and a ceremonial meat fork were tucked into an outer fold. And inside, the bundle held glass beads from a dance belt, a grass mat, and several symbols of warriors wrapped in individual leather pouches: a bald eagle talon and the skulls and skins of eight hawks and falcons.

The bundle had belonged to a family rather than their tribe, but tribal bundles across the Plains told similar stories, of the sacred visions and rituals of the people. One of the Pawnees' tribal bundles, for example, carried the story of a village's origins. Another told of the sacred buffalo skull. The Big Black Meteoric Star bundle presided over cleansing rituals before the bison hunt. Only men performed the associated rituals, but the bundles were passed down from mother to daughter.

No one knows the vision story of the bundle in the museum. That story, long treasured, was lost in a single afternoon, in the place now called Massacre Canyon.

The summer bison hunt of 1873 had been good for the Skidi, Kitkehahki, Tsawi, and Pitahawirata people, the four bands of the Pawnees. They knew that the star Canopus would soon appear in the southern sky, time for harvest. So the people were headed home.

Since 1859 home had meant a reservation in southern Nebraska along the banks of the North Loup River. But for the seven hundred years before that, the bands had lived in villages scattered along the Loup, Platte, and Republican rivers in what would become Nebraska and northern Kansas. The people had been sustained by the gifts of earth and sky: duck, quail, fish, antelope, buffalo, elk, turtles, and river clams. Wild plums and strawberries, calamus, ground nuts, and sunflowers. Pawnee women even gathered the hog peanut from the nest of the tiny vole, leaving something in exchange so the mice children wouldn't starve.

Each summer and winter for centuries, the people of the four bands packed up their skin tents and poles, cooking pots and food, and left to follow the buffalo herds. A thousand or more women, children, and warriors, together with their pack horses, traveled as far west and south as the Solomon River in Kansas at the rate of ten miles a day. On the return journey they were even more heavily laden with the fruits of the hunt: buffalo skins for making clothes, blankets, and moccasins; sinews for thread; bones for hoes, scythes, spoons, and other tools; and enough dried meat to last the season.

Altogether, the people were away from their villages for two months or more. Meanwhile, during the summer, the old and infirm ones, left at home, tended the crops ripening along the river bottoms. Squashes, melons, beans, and a rainbow assortment of corn—green, blue, spotted, white, yellow, red, sweet, and Osage—would help fill the larders for winter.

By late August the people would return. They burned sage to freshen the lodges, then stored their tons of meat and hides. For the next three weeks, the women brought in the harvest and prepared it for storage. They roasted or dried the ears of corn, then pried off the kernels; scorched and peeled the pumpkin shells, saving the seeds for the next year and weaving mats from the strips of dried pumpkin meat. They also dried the beans and beat them from their shells with sticks and winnowed them in the wind. Finally, they gathered the summer's wild fruits—strawberries, ground cherries, and yellow plums—to dry, eat raw, or make into jelly. In good years, between the harvest and the hunt, every lodge's storage pit, eight feet deep, was filled to the brim.

And so the year went round. After harvest came the October festivals and Grand Doctors' ceremonies filled with performances, processions, and mime shows. In fall and spring the women wove straw mats, sewed clothes and moccasins, and made skin coverings for tepees and tents. In December the people left again on the winter hunt, and in March, sowed new crops.

By 1873 many things had changed. Besieged by enemy tribes, attacked by white settlers, deprived of land, and decimated by alien diseases, the Pawnees—once the most powerful tribe on the plains—had suffered many losses. Since the height of the Colorado gold rush and the start of the Civil War, the strain had been immense. Traffic on westward trails had scattered the buffalo and pushed the Pawnees' enemies, Oglalas and Brules—two bands of the Tetons—to more desperate acts of encroachment. Like other Native peoples, the Pawnees had repeatedly given up land, left their traditional village sites, and moved ever smaller numbers into ever shrinking space. From a population of thirty thousand in 1800, only twenty-five hundred remained.

By this time, too, the U.S. government had grouped the four

bands together and labeled them the "Pawnees." The move simpli-
fied treaty talks and "management," but the name was foreign to the
bands' self-understanding. They called themselves *Chahiksichahiks*,
"men of men." The name "Pawnee" came from the language of
their enemy, the Tetons. It means "alien people."

The 1873 hunt began as it always had, though the Pawnees now
had to ask government permission to leave the reservation, only
five hundred people planned to travel, and the range of the hunt
had shrunk. This time, they would journey no farther than western
Nebraska. They also had to be escorted by government trail agents,
who also provided some measure of protection. This, the government had promised in exchange for the concession of Pawnee lands.
This time, however, the government also supplied the Tetons with
firearms and allowed them to leave their reservation at the same
time. This hunt would be the Pawnees' last.

The plains in late August can broil, with temperatures above one
hundred. Near Frenchman's Creek in southwestern Nebraska, it was
midafternoon when Pawnee women set about the long-practiced
choreography of slicing, drying, and packing buffalo meat and hides.
Even on a large hunt, a hundred women, helped by many of the
men and girls, could prepare all the meat, organs, sinew, and bone
in only a few hours. Even children helped. That year, they included
a five-year-old Kitkehahki girl whose white name was Sadie.

During the many weeks of the hunt, Sadie had played with other
children and swum in the creeks. She might even have taken the
papery husk of the ground cherry, as Pawnee children liked to do,
and popped it on her forehead, laughing. Their game gave the
ground cherry its name, *nikaktspak* (forehead, to pop). And perhaps
she had laughed and tried to trip the old doctor when, prancing like a
buffalo, he danced through the camp chanting, "Now you are going
to trot / Buffalo who are killed falling." Now at Frenchman's Creek,
she worked beside her mother, grandmothers, and aunts preparing
for the hunters to bring back their kill.

Some women set up drying racks and put water on to boil for

curing the buffalo heart, tongue, and entrails. Others stretched and scraped hides, or sliced the meat, lungs, and heart into strips to dry. Still others cracked and boiled the bones for the fat, extracting and saving the marrow. The workers also washed, boiled, and dried the animals' intestines.

According to trail agent John Williamson, although the formal hunts had ended, Pawnee warriors had ridden out after a few stragglers. Sky Chief felled his animal first and had begun to butcher it when he found himself surrounded by Teton warriors, Oglala and Brule. Another Pawnee warrior, who saw Sky Chief die, escaped to warn the people. Quickly they herded the pack horses into a shallow, nearby canyon. Sadie huddled behind her parents.

While the Pawnees had only bows and arrows and the Tetons carried guns, the Pawnees outnumbered their enemies. Women chanted war songs above the clamor; for a while, the fighters held the Tetons off. Then suddenly the hundred attackers became a thousand, all of them armed and firing into the canyon.

Retreat. The Pawnees cut the leather packs from their horses, dropping six tons of goods to the canyon floor—all their winter provisions. Amid the firing guns and shouting, with horses and people falling around them, Sadie's parents lifted her onto a horse and strapped their sacred medicine bundle to her back. If she took care of it, they said, it would always protect her. Then they slapped the horse, sending it racing away.

Sadie's parents died at Massacre Canyon along with more than a hundred other Pawnees. Eleven women and children disappeared as Teton captives. Sadie and her cousin Nellie escaped.

Those who eluded the slaughter had lost their household goods and summer kill. Back at the North Loup, as they would soon find, their crops had been decimated by potato beetles and locusts. The Pawnees, who had endured losing their land and rivers, their autonomy, their power, and tens of thousands of their people, finally lost heart. For years they had resisted government pressure to give up Nebraska altogether. But now they agreed to go.

Over the next two years, they migrated to Oklahoma on foot, carrying seeds and cuttings of wild plum in their sacred bundles. Seven hundred people died along the way. Five hundred more died in the first five years of resettlement. By 1883, ten years after Massacre Canyon, half a million white settlers had poured into Nebraska. The 1910 census counted 633 Pawnees—including Sadie, who had traveled into exile with her tribe, still carrying her sacred bundle.

Nearly a hundred years later, a Pawnee woman named Dolly stopped by the Kitkehahki village on her way to Nebraska. She circled the lodge floor and studied the artifacts, and told the story of her family's sacred bundle. At age five she had inherited the bundle when her mother died of a spider bite. And Dolly decided that, when she died and her family could no longer care for it, the bundle should go to the museum.

And so it was. For Dolly's mother was Sadie, the girl who fled Massacre Canyon in 1873 with the sacred bundle on her back. Though its vision story is lost, its rituals unremembered, Sadie's family bundle came home in 1987 to the village of the Kitkehahki band.

The story of that bundle has stayed with me a long time. When I think of the lodge and the grounds and the bluffs and the sun-blanched view from the Kitkehahki village, I think mostly of Sadie. Perhaps because I want to see myself in the daughter who out of sacred duty preserved her family talismans; and because, even though so much of the story is lost, the tale of their rescue creates a thread that links generations. Or maybe because, in encountering Sadie, I was learning the connection between place and the stories that give it meaning, just as the bundle stories tied people to the spirits of the land.

The other part of the story that stays with me is the image of the people leaving their land—women, children, warriors, elders, gathering their belongings and starting out on the arduous trek to Oklahoma. I think back to the Ute elder in Colorado who had said,

"When you live in a place for a long time, you think that way"; and I know that when the people left Nebraska, they left a place that had shaped both their thought and who they were. But in their violent uprooting, they also carried something vital with them: stories, tribal ways, a world of belief marked by the patterns of the sky, and cuttings of wild plum. All signs of their relation to place that had been rooted, grounded and growing. Signs that, when planted in the earth in a new place, would give them sustenance and some small link of continuity and remembrance.

The first time I left San Francisco for Kansas, I went in search of the sites and shreds of my family story. But now I began to see that, to have a sense of place, I needed more. Something more akin to the wild plums.

I felt the same when I stood before the Pawnee star chart at the museum. The tawny skin, covered by hundreds of small black x's, came from the Skidi band of the Pawnees—often called the sky people, astronomers of the plains. A circular horizon line suggests the dome of the heavens, and the x's map the night sky.

We non-Pawnees know that star charts record the wisdom and stories of the heavens and creation, of the star gods and the cycles of life. Constellations like the Little Duck and the Big Duck and the one we call the Pleiades tell when to plant, when to hunt, and when to harvest. Polaris, the largest star, protects the tribe. The Milky Way, which pours down the center of the star map, divides the year. But like other Native American maps, star charts illustrate oral records. And like the bundle's vision story, those records were lost in the bad times, when the keepers of the stories died.

I wanted to understand it, but the sky map spoke a language I didn't know. I felt I was standing on the verge of some new clarity, something I had sought since first setting out across the Rockies some two years before with the ghosts of my parents in tow. Like Sadie's bundle and the wild plums, the star chart suggested a widening frame of reference, a deepening sense of place.

Looking back, I could trace this moment to the start of my first

Kansas sojourn, at the Colorado History Museum in Denver. There, I peered into ledger drawings by the elite Cheyenne warriors known as Dog Soldiers. Across the lined ledger pages, warriors rode horses with lean, stylized bodies and necks and small, elegant heads. A splash of red suggested a cavalry officer's wounds; a feather or fringe or weapon marked a warrior. The drawings recounted stories of strategy and courage, victories in warfare and wounds bravely borne. In one, Red Lance stands arrayed for battle, his body painted yellow on instructions from the gods. In another, he has painted buffalo tracks on his leg and face, a half moon on his chest—emblems of divine protection.

I had known almost nothing about the Cheyennes before that day. Of course, I'd seen my share of westerns and had learned enough to know that movies lied. I knew about forced assimilation and genocide. But I'd never felt it viscerally. Now the drawings pulled me so far into that Cheyenne world that, for the first time, I could look out at my own from the other side. From the Others' side. Here was a culture with a fully evolved set of values, standards of valor, and rules of engagement. A world that saw itself in its own terms, a world worth dying for. And even if all the coups in all the ledger books on the plains could not finally defeat the U.S. government, the Dog Soldiers had continued to fight for their land and way of life. They had fought to avenge Sand Creek. I'd learned that story then for the first time, too.

On an early November morning in 1864, Colonel John Chivington and some 650 volunteer militiamen rode quietly toward a camp of Cheyennes and Arapahos along Sand Creek, about a mile north of Dawson's Bend. The soldiers saw the American colors flying from the camp and watched the people come out to greet them with gestures of peace. Black Kettle, after all, had been promised that his band would be safe at Sand Creek. But at Chivington's signal, the soldiers began firing. Three howitzers and hundreds of fire-arms obliterated the camp. The rampaging soldiers bashed in the skulls of crying children. They raped and murdered the women. A month later, the victims' genitals were paraded across the stage of the Denver Opera House.

The city, led to believe that Chivington had cleared Sand Creek of hostile Indians, declared a holiday and feted him with a parade.

Chivington's victory didn't last. Before long, soldiers who had refused to join in the killings began to talk. The subsequent congressional investigation and military tribunal both condemned Chivington and his men. Still, the atrocities went unpunished. Chivington retired to Nebraska and had a Colorado town named in his honor. It still sits on the plains of southeastern Colorado, a ghost town laid out along the Santa Fe tracks, a handful of miles from the massacre site. In 2007, after decades of struggle against local opposition, a national park opened there, dedicated to the Cheyenne and Arapaho dead.

The year after seeing the Cheyenne drawings, I'd driven again from Denver to Kansas, this time taking a detour through the remnants of Chivington, then down a graveled county road toward Sand Creek. No signs announced the turnoff, and the National Park Service hadn't yet begun its work. Though I could see it, I couldn't reach the site. Where the road ended, I stood at a barbed wire fence looking out across wide pastures, empty of people, of buildings, of cattle, silent but for crickets, a bird. I could see all the way to where the dry creek bed carved a pale scar across the land.

There, watching the wind trouble the grass, seeing that scar, I didn't know why I'd felt compelled to come. Maybe I had hoped it would answer the question that the ledger drawings had raised. What should a white, middle-class woman in America do with such a story? Or the one about the Puritan Robert Seeley, my first ancestor in America. He'd sailed from London in 1630 with his wife Mary (née Mason), who, somewhere in the middle of the Atlantic, gave birth to a son. After landing in Massachusetts, they moved on to Connecticut, where Robert Seeley and his sons, and lord knows how many other Seeleys—their names litter plaques all over New England—would fight Indians and found towns, including Quinnipiac colony, founded in 1639.

Robert Seeley, Quinnipiac's marshal, appears often in the town's early records. For example, he's named as a witness in the trial proceedings of a man arrested for having sexual relations with a pig. Less winningly, on October 30, 1639, Seeley ordered that a local Indian named Nepaupuk, convicted of murder, be punished by decapitation and that, as a warning to other Natives, his head be "pitched upon a pole" on the village green. The name of Nepaupuk's tribe is not recorded. The next year, Quinnipiac was renamed "New Haven."

For five years, I walked across that village green every day on my way to class.

Where do guilt and responsibility lie? I owe my daily walk across the New Haven Green and much of my good fortune to Robert Seeley and Mary. Not only because they braved the Atlantic to build the city on a hill and proved fecund in the New World. But also because Robert Seeley helped clear the Connecticut woods of Pequots, Quiripis, and Mohegans.

Sand Creek, New Haven, San Francisco—where the Spanish military enslaved the Ohlone in that year of liberty, 1776. Virtually every American place has a similar story. Racial violence has seeped, like smoke, into the fabric of our culture; it marks who we are. My French, Norwegian, English, and Irish forebears planted dreams in Wisconsin, Michigan, Canada, and California, in soil made virgin through plunder. They put down roots where others' had been yanked up.

So where does that leave me? Because I have profited from the displacement of Native tribes, am I responsible for what happened to the Pequots? Or to the Cheyennes, the Ohlones, the Osage?

White students of mine sometimes squirm when confronted with the anger of minority writers, especially those who protest historical wrongs. When I taught Jamaica Kincaid's "On Seeing England for the First Time" in a course on rhetoric and culture, one student bristled. He "disagreed" with Kincaid's anger, the anger of a black Antiguan who had been expected to mimic the superior customs, honor the weightier history, and worship the white skin of England. I took this student's disagreement to mean that he felt unjustly accused. Made guilty for belonging to the white, Euro-American world. Colonial oppression ended a long time ago, he said. Kincaid should get over it.

It was one of those teaching moments that didn't lead to magic. No light bulbs went on; we didn't finish class filled with love and understanding. I blame myself. I tried to reason. First of all, I told him, colonialism doesn't work like that, here one day, gone the next. Culture is complex—causes have effects that last. My student still disagreed. Class went on in a muddled, tense way, the other students unwilling to speak their minds, all of us paralyzed by the fearful topic of race and cultural guilt.

If I'd been more on my game, less confused about how to clear the path without shutting up the one student who dared to speak, I would have focused not on his disagreement but on his anger. Why, I would have asked the class, might we feel angry in response to Kincaid's essay? Is it because we feel accused of being who we are and of things we haven't done? If a long sequence of forces and events beyond our control results in privileges we never asked for, are we responsible? And if so, in what way?

If I had known the story of Nepaupuk then, I would have talked about being Robert Seeley's granddaughter, many greats- down the line. Of course, I didn't fire a musket at Pequots in Connecticut. I didn't order Nepaupuk to be killed, his head displayed on a pike. I didn't force the Osage to abandon their children's graves in Wichita. Of these things, I am innocent.

Though I'm not responsible for those events, I can still be responsible to them. I can listen to the suffering and anger of the conquered and displaced and to their heirs; I can bear witness. I can listen with an expansive heart, undefended, knowing that I belong to the story, too.

We are all knit together, the descendants of the vanquished and the victors, the enslaved and the free, those who occupied the land and those who lost it. The same nation that sent Robert Seeley to

America also colonized Jamaica Kincaid's island, transporting Africans to work there as slaves. My family's houses in Wichita occupied Osage hunting grounds. If I am to know those places that have housed, nurtured, and entertained me, I can learn their histories. And learn them from more sides than one.

Otherwise, how do I know where I am? Or who I am?

So I've continued learning those stories. But standing in front of the Pawnee star chart, I also heard a whisper of something else. A need to not only learn the stories, but learn from them. Native history is more than the story of dislocation, uprooting, and violence. It is a repository of ways of seeing the world that are different from anything most Western, industrial people know. I knew I was at the edge of learning something: a deeper, richer way to map my place, a different way to belong.

The day before coming to the Kitkehahki village, I'd gotten lost inside a medicine wheel. A collaboration between students at Haskell Indian Nations University in Lawrence and Kansas crop artist Stan Herd, the wheel had been mown into the tall grass on the edge of the Haskell campus.

I park the car a short distance away and walk down a grassy alley and into the wheel. I can tell it's a circle, a large circle, but I can't really make out the design. The sun is bearing down on my arms and neck—it's at least one hundred degrees . . . the grass is tinder-box dry . . . I think I must have circled all the way around but suddenly find myself inside a smaller circle, then in a clearing where two slender poles stand topped with feathers . . . more circling, more clearings. Monoliths in some of them, large stones in others, pennies and wrapped chewing gum laid on top. Offerings . . . I circle, circle . . . here are the stones again . . . the feather-topped poles. But are they the same ones? Is this the same circle or a different one? Around . . . more stones. Where's the path to the outer edge? Faster, walking . . . How do I get out?

My old fear—lost—flickers to life. A low flame, but still. How silly. I left my car not two minutes away, at the end of a tree-lined, mown-grass alley. How hard can it be to get out? I abandon the path and cut straight across the pattern, scratching my shins on the dry, spiky grass. Where did this cluster of trees come from? I didn't pass them on my way in. Where is my car?

I am still a daughter of latitude and longitude. I still feel a flutter of panic if I don't know my way. It reminds me of a story from a Native American tradition that the poet David Whyte tells. A little boy asks an elder, "What do I do if I am lost in the forest?" And the elder replies, "Stop and look around you. For the trees are not lost."

The trees are not lost. Neither is the sun or the stars or the phases of the moon. Nature is not lost. Look around you. I take a deep breath and stand still. Stop walking and pay attention. Look at the sun. Late afternoon. Sun's in the west. To go north, keep the sun on your left.

Ten seconds later, I was back in the alley; and in two minutes, my car.

If I had known its language, I could have taken my directions from the medicine wheel. A printed guide I picked up later explains. The wheel maps the universe, taking its shape from the sacred circle. The sacred hoop, the medicine wheel, the mound, the earth lodge, the village, the cycles of the seasons, the movements of the sun, the orbs of earth and sky. Even the roundness of a bird's nest, Black Elk says. They all remind us of the interconnection of all things. They remind us who and where we are.

From my human-eye level, I couldn't see the medicine wheel. But I could have, from the sky. Spokes inside the circle point in the four directions. Their end points, the feathered poles, mark nature's balance and the summer and winter solstices. Deer prints at north and south signify the sacred path within the seasons. The monoliths represent the four grandfathers; the stone cairns, the movement of the stars.

The guide goes on: "We undertake this sharing to teach a lesson about our relationship to the places we live. . . . We are all related in the overlapping circles that embody the complex web of life."

The circles in which I'd felt lost were not meant to trick or entangle me, but to weave me in. To map my place in relation to all things.

Inside the medicine wheel, before the Pawnee star chart, in the story of Sadie's sacred bundle, in the cuttings of wild plum, I knew I had encountered something vital. Something that in all my travels, along with family stories, I had been trying to recover. Our dislocation had been family upheaval and a culture-wide unmooring. Unrooted, our pole stars unknown, our seasons marked by firing up the furnace or turning up the AC, by semesters and summer vacation. Our food apparently growing in the aisles of the grocery store. What I wanted, but couldn't yet articulate, was a connection to place that planted me in the earth.

....

CHAPTER EIGHT

What the Prairie Teaches

A friend said I just had to stop in and meet Wes Jackson outside Salina, smack-dab in the center of Kansas, so I thought, why not? Another Kansas adventure, a lark. So when I pulled into the gravel parking lot of the Land Institute, I couldn't guess that an hour later I'd drive away elated and changed. The deeper sense of place I had been longing for was waiting in the roots of the prairie.

Wes pulled up, grinning out the window of his dark blue Japanese car.

"Are you ready for me?" he asked. He had a shock of white hair; large, friendly features; and a manner both impish and imperious. I didn't know. Was I ready?

"Get in," he said.

We drove down a short gravel road, with Wes pointing out the experimental farm plots, greenhouse, barn, and scattering of buildings that make up the Land Institute. Everyone calls it the Land.

Almost as soon as we'd started, we stopped, pulling up to a house you might find in the bayside hills north of San Francisco, say in Sausalito. A two-story box with an upstairs deck and a grapevine twined around the railing. I hadn't expected any of it, least of all the grapevine. "It reminds us of Tuscany," he explained. "We love it there. And my wife designed the house. Big, open kitchen. She's from California." My mind shifted gears, trying to fit this big Kansan into Tuscany, and a Californian who designed her own house into

Kansas. Before I could ask, or even wonder, Wes added, "She loves it here in Kansas."

We stood in the yard on a patch of lawn surrounded by tallgrass prairie and the ditzy buzz and hop of insect life. Wes showed me where the Smoky Hill River ran behind the house at the bottom of a steep decline, making its way east from Colorado toward Junction City. There it would join the Republican and become the Kansas, which empties into the Missouri, which flows into the Mississippi. Like other rivers flowing east out of the Rockies, its waters eventually end up in the Gulf of Mexico. Here at the Land, the river forms part of the Smoky Hill–Saline River basin, where it cuts through crop land and pastures that are sometimes flat and sometimes not. Just to the east, the Flint Hills begin. Wes had landed in a gorgeous spot, no question. I told him so.

"Well, don't tell anybody," he said. "They all think it's nothing but flat here, that we're all just a bunch of slack-jawed prairie billies." He laughed. The prejudice doesn't bother him. It keeps out the riffraff.

Wes pointed to a merry-go-round planted at the edge of the lawn. He had rescued it from a defunct grade school. Nice, I thought, a bit of history for his grandchildren, saved from the trash heap. Four flat metal seats sat at the ends of a four-armed X, each with a little handle to hold.

"Get on," he said. Oh god.

We perched like giants on our tiny seats, knees up, heels jammed over the crossbars. I looked at Wes for instruction. "Let's go," he said. I gripped my handle and leaned back, pulled, leaned forward, pushed. I pushed, Wes pulled, the merry-go-round began to turn. Pushing and pulling, back and forth, we started to speed, the seesawing growing fast and easy. I felt a little giddy. Merry. I grinned. I wanted to throw my head back and watch the sky spin.

"Now watch the middle," Wes said.

Straining to hold my head up, I tried to focus. As the merry-go-round went round, the center axle turned.

Wes planted his foot in the grass, dragging us to a stop. "Now get off," he said.

Now, what? I unfolded my limbs and climbed off, dizzy. I wobbled, tried to find my footing. I could see the headlines. Interviewer falls on face after riding child's toy. Wes stayed on and got the thing going again.

"Watch the middle," he said. The yard kept spinning, but I managed to find the axle. Wes orbited, but this time the axle didn't move.

"Ah," I said, glimpsing something, reaching for a reason. My head felt woozy. Wes braked and hopped off, steady as a pioneer.

"And that," he said triumphantly, "was Galileo's problem with the church."

I laughed. Of course. Your paradigm depends on where you stand. All my training in post-structuralism boiled down to the merry-go-round.

"Let's sit," he said, gesturing at two metal garden chairs near the house. I took a step and stumbled.

"Are you okay?" Wes took my elbow and guided me across the lawn.

"You are on the earth when you're on the merry-go-round. Now the church said, 'God wouldn't fool us.' But Galileo saw that perception is not always truth. You have to step outside the system to see things differently."

In the spirit of Galileo, Wes had started the Land. He'd gotten off the merry-go-round to take a fresh look at the world.

He pulled the chairs into the shade of the honey locust tree. At nine in the morning, it was already ninety-five and sultry.

He launched into the history of the Land, beginning with his great-grandfather, who rode into Kansas "with the white tide," as he put it, in 1854. That makes Wes a fourth generation Kansan, steeped in his ancestral values of frugality and stewardship of the land. Those virtues eventually led him to earn a PhD in genetics and start the environmental studies program at California State, Sacramento. He eventually came back to Kansas to homestead with his children, and in 1978 he started the Land. Though he left a plum academic job to do it, he continues to teach—to interns, colleagues, farmers, any audience he can get ahold of. Me.

Explaining what they do at the Land, he invoked not only Galileo but Copernicus, Descartes, Bacon, Newton, Darwin, and Shakespeare; and he quoted from their works, including Pope's "Letter to Burlington." Wes was clearly a literary and metaphorical thinker, given to the quick analogies, illustrations, aphorisms, and jokes of a gifted teacher. And the passion of a benevolent zealot.

The work, he explained, began with the prairie and ended with a radical thought. Radical, as in roots. The prairie sustains itself without human intervention. Its deep root systems conserve the soil and preserve plants from drought. More than simple grass, the prairie contains dozens of species—grasses, sedges, and forbs—in an interdependent system of mutual aid.

I could tell he'd explained it all a thousand times, but it still seemed fresh, important. The prospect of winning a new soul enlivened him. "The prairie runs on rain and sunlight," Wes said. Period. No annual plowing or planting, no soil stripped bare by harvest. No synthetic pesticides or fertilizers. No petrofuel required. The prairie's natural system had inspired him to ask, why can't we grow food the same way?

That question drives research at the Land. The goal is perennial, polyculture farming, with mixed species in the same field, all of them self-renewing. No more miles and miles of wheat alone, alfalfa, soybeans, or corn. Wes explained the basic mix of plants— cold weather grass, warm weather grass, sunflower, and legume. Like the prairie. The mix keeps nutrients in the soil, and the roots keep the soil on the land.

The lecture rolled on, sweeping me up in the tide. The great plow up of the late nineteenth and early twentieth centuries destroyed most of the continent's prairie ecosystems. And that led to the Dust Bowl, when, in the space of a few years, 85 million tons of topsoil, no longer held down by sod, blew away in the wind. It's still going where it doesn't belong. Wes gestured toward the muddy Smoky Hill behind us. "There's our nation's wealth, headed to the Gulf of Mexico. Millions of acres, down the drain." In an untouched prairie-only watershed, even during torrential rains, rivers and creeks run clear.

I felt overwhelmed by information but also excited by the simplicity and promise of it all, the brilliance of applying the prairie's know-how to growing food and saving soil. But Wes and the Land's researchers aim to save more than that. Agriculture that works without petroleum-based fertilizers, pesticides, or tractor fuel, he went on, will improve farmers' physical and fiscal health and will end the drain that carries not only Midwest soils but polluted runoff into the Mississippi. In the Gulf of Mexico, that runoff has created a dead zone the size of New Jersey. A place so saturated with nitrogen and depleted of oxygen that marine animals flee if they can, and suffocate if they can't. Saving agriculture could help save the planet. The problems and possibilities seemed equally huge. I was hooked.

While Wes talked, we strolled from the yard down to the Land, where all the work was happening. We stopped in front of a trial plot of something that looked a lot like corn, with tall stalks and long pliable leaves. "Sorghum," Wes told me. In the states, it feeds cattle; but in Africa, it's a staple food. He pointed to the tips of the stalks and their clusters of rust-colored, berrylike grains. "That would be useful in Africa, don't you think?" I agreed it would. It would also save African farmers from the corporations trying to colonize African agriculture with the promise of petrochemicals and patented, GMO crops. Chemical inputs cost money and damage the land, he went on; but even worse, the farmers can't save GMO seeds for the next year's crop. Genetic engineering makes saving seeds for next year's crop either pointless, because it renders the seeds infertile after one generation, or illegal unless the farmers pay expensive royalties. The whole business clearly angered Wes. He views his sorghum through a different lens. Labor-saving, people-saving agriculture whose bottom line is measured by its benefit to communities and the environment. Not to corporations.

We stopped again near the greenhouse, where Wes pulled a shock of prairie grass from a white pvc tube that had been stuck in the ground. He held it up high to show me the full length of its tangled, hairy roots. They were at least as long as I was tall—about six feet. No wonder they kept water and soil in place. The roots of conventional wheat, a cultivated annual grass, Wes explained, could be measured in inches. All those years I'd lived in Kansas, and clearly, I knew nothing. In thirty minutes I had become a new recruit of natural systems farming—organic, sustainable, petroleum free.

Wes said the work feels urgent, and not because he was aging. "I don't expect to live to see this vision fully realized," he said, "but you don't plant a sapling for yourself, you plant it for your grandchildren." It's urgent because the planet's in a perilous state. We've burned more than half the world's oil in the past seventy-five years. The Fossil Fuel Age—like the Stone, Bronze, or Iron ages before it—will end. Not might, but will. I suddenly felt the urgency myself. It seemed a stunning thought. What would such a future look like?

"When that happens," he said, "we'll all become Methodists." He laughed. "There will be discipline, austerity, frugality." But once the Land successfully breeds its perennial crops—not through genetic modification but cross-pollination and "embryo rescue"—we may become Methodists, but we will also have food. "We're a huge pro-life operation," he joked. "Embryo rescue is all we do."

The tour ended and we stood in the parking lot. Pointing to a spot at the edge of the gravel, Wes described the mural he envisioned for The Land. "It will go right here," he said. Just beyond it, a field of unplowed prairie covered the hill. "By the way, we're going to put buffalo there." The mural would depict Galileo, Copernicus, Descartes, Bacon, Newton, Darwin, and Henry A. Wallace, secretary of agriculture under FDR and the first U.S. public advocate for ecology. Wallace has inspired, among other groups, Greenpeace. And above these figures, Wes envisions Eve with the snake and the apple being expelled from the garden by the flaming sword.

I wondered where this Bible talk would lead, but also knew enough by now not to assume anything. The analogy began to bloom. Eve is forbidden the Tree of Life, he explained, when she gains the Tree of Knowledge. We're also in danger of losing the Tree of Life, enamored of our own knowledge. Wes insisted we have to subordinate knowledge to life if we're going to save the planet. The Tree of Life gives us, for example, the prairie. It teaches nature's best way. The Tree of Knowledge produces the Land's experimental plots, the application of science to nature. So knowledge isn't the enemy. But when we assume in our hubris that we know enough to act—following Descartes in believing that our knowledge is sufficient—we get a world like the one we live in now. But when we accept our ignorance, we are cautious, slow to act. We measure the exits. We take our time. Wes was planning an Ignorant World Views Conference in honor of this fact. "It's our strong suit, ignorance," he said. "We ought to go with it." We both laughed. I felt my paradigm shifting out from under me.

For years, I'd mouthed the right words about ecology; I'd gardened without pesticides and decried global warming. To protect biodiversity, I'd paid two dollars for an heirloom tomato. I'd recycled. But I hadn't before felt how connected we all are to farming. Agriculture didn't just happen in the flyover zone. It happened on my urban table, on the tables of Africans, in the water, the air, the Gulf of Mexico.

It had taken a long time for Western science to catch up with ancient wisdom. I hadn't yet made the connection; but here at the Land, the Pawnee star map and the Haskell earthworks would be at home. Lost in the forest? Look around you. The trees are not lost. Lost in the twenty-first century? Want to survive the coming end of the Fossil Fuel Age? Look around you. The prairie is not lost. Its deep tangled roots can show us what we need to know. Can teach us how to live, by observing and honoring the natural systems of the world. I wasn't yet sure how deeply this idea could apply to my life, but I knew somehow that it would. I had found what I needed to cultivate a sense of place that went deeper than stories, right down into the soil.

Opening my car door, I asked if I could buy organic produce anywhere in Salina. Wes laughed. Apparently not.

"Have you been able to eat here in Kansas?" He looked quizzical and teasing.

"Well, that's been a bit of a problem," I ventured, assuming he would sympathize.

"You look like you've lost weight." I bristled. Not the response I'd hoped for. But coming from Wes, it also sounded innocuous, like a remark about the weather. "You're about as skinny as a matchstick," he added. Looks like rain.

Absurdly, defensively, I kept the conversation going. "I think I've actually gained a few pounds." How could I not? Nothing but road food for the past week, no exercise. Not to mention the big, fat dinner I'd eaten the night before at Grandma Max's truck stop. My rare Kansas indulgence. Chicken-fried steak with gravy, mashed potatoes, green beans simmered with bacon for hours, and cherry pie à la mode. I had loved every fat-dripping bite. But it was a tough meal for a salad eater. I'd spent a bloated night awake, staring at the ceiling. I didn't mention that to Wes. Wanting to convince him that I wasn't such a hothouse flower, that I'd really put on pounds, I added, "I haven't been exercising like I do at home."

"Oh, that's right," he laughed. "You people exercise." I laughed, too. People only exercise if they've no real work to do. Wes had work to do. I watched him waving in my rear view mirror. I waved back. He turned back to the Land.

Two nights later, I dreamt of prairie grass. Seas of it tossing its head in waves, bowing down, running through the fingers of the wind. There was no road in my dream, no car. I felt as though I were flying beside fields of grass, like my recurring dream in the fifth grade, in which I flew to school four feet above the sidewalk, working hard to keep aloft, urging myself on past every crack in the sidewalk, every splintery telephone pole.

In this new dream, though, flying came without effort. Without noise. Like a movie without sound. No conflict, no rising action, no crisis or denouement. None of the surreal logic of dreams, no absurd collages or leaps across time. Only grass and a view of grass, gold, brown, ripe and blowing, fields bathed in sunlight.

In *My Ántonia* Jim Burden lies down in the tall grass of the prairie and feels "entirely happy." He speculates that "perhaps we feel like that when we die and become part of something entire, whether it is sun or air, or goodness and knowledge. At any rate, that is happiness; to be dissolved into something complete and great." In my dream, I had dissolved into something complete and great, beyond self, beyond body, beyond ego, beyond time.

I awoke befuddled, with a pillow over my eyes. The rhythm of the road still ran beneath my senses, and I tried to remember where I was and where I'd be driving that day. I pulled the pillow off my face. Cars taking the shortcut from Market Street were jamming outside my window, swerving around cyclists and double-parked cars, honking their way through the morning. I laughed. San Francisco. Home.

With the feeling of the dream still alive on my skin, I thought, what if I were to choose Kansas? Couldn't I live there? Not always, but part of the year. Have a summer place with a creek and wildflowers, a place to write. A dacha. Why not? Frederick and I were about to be married, and he might even love the idea. Would he? Of course, I'd be realistic. I knew that if Willa Cather had ever lain in the tall grass as Jim Burden did, a dozen chiggers would have dug in beneath the elastic of her bloomers. I also knew that because of work, I would only be able to go in summer, just in time for tornadoes and heatstroke. Or at Christmas break, ten below. But still, I'd have the prairie, the horizon, the sunsets, the sky.

I began reading my way through the stack of books Wes had handed me at the Land. "Here, take this," he'd said, piling on another one. "Take this, too." I'd ended up with *Farming in Nature's Image* and

New Roots for Agriculture, and a couple of years' worth of Land Institute reports. I settled on Wes's own *Becoming Native to This Place*. Both the title and the idea appealed to me. Could I become, at last, native to Kansas?

Becoming Native retraced what I'd heard at the Land. But the last chapter turned from plant to human communities. One sentence stopped me. "It seems that we still blunt our sensitivities about our local places by the likes of learning long passages from *The Aeneid* while wanting to shake from us the dust of Red Cloud or Matfield Green." I balked. What's wrong with *The Aeneid*? I backed up. The remark followed one from Wallace Stegner, who thought that Willa Cather wrote better novels when she stuck to Red Cloud, Nebraska, and worse ones when she decided against the place she came from. When she put on the cloak of European culture as if it were the only one that mattered.

I felt caught in the headlights of a new idea. Or saw my earlier hostility toward Kansas anew, as a historical, national habit. All of us refugees—Cather, San Franciscans, me—we'd all shaken off the dust of Red Cloud or Dubuque or Woonsocket, South Dakota, and put on other forms of culture as though the one we came from didn't count. As though it had nothing to do with who we were.

I celebrated San Francisco's uniqueness and cheered when the Italian neighborhood North Beach fought off Burger King and when the city banned big box stores. I refused to go to Starbucks, since it displaced local businesses and erased local charm. In proud, resistant San Francisco, I decried Wes's notion of blunted sensitivities to the local—a blindness that was homogenizing culture everywhere. The same suburbs, same stores in the same malls, same green lawns no matter the climate. Same corporate economy running on money and oil. I could scornfully recite the litany of the American landscape: Days Inn, Sleep Inn, Wendy's, McDonald's, Applebee's, Walmart, Kmart, PetSmart. Welcome to anyplace.

In San Francisco the argument had seemed obvious. But my determined embrace of the city—and its treasures for me had been many and real—had also entailed a willful denigration of the place I had left. I had thought of Kansas as not San Francisco, without a value of its own.

The idea of becoming Kansan again—or for the first time—took on the persuasiveness of metaphor. Could I wear both cloaks, of Kansas and San Francisco, the Big Arkansas and the Pacific Rim, tornado alley and Oz, *My Ántonia*, and *The Aeneid*? Couldn't I love, and live in, both?

Wes thinks people should read *The Aeneid*. The man who cites Shakespeare to explain sorghum could hardly oppose the author of the *Georgics*. We should read it, he writes, not to "adorn [our] talk, to show off, but . . . for insight, for utility, as well as for pleasure." But he thinks people should also dwell in the particularities of their own place. Build community not around a single paradigm but around what the place itself offers and requires. He cites Henry Wallace, who argues that "Every community can become something distinctly precious in its own right."

Clearly, I'd brought back more from the Land than a new enthusiasm about agriculture. I was beginning to see how the many threads of my journey intertwined: Community. Earth. Stories. Roots. A sense of place required the lore and the wild plums, the stars and the seasons, and people who shared a common life. Different in every location, essential everywhere. All the things I'd missed growing up. I felt ready for it all.

In Wes's world, bringing all these threads together requires "agriculture with a human face." A model of farming that helps rural communities cultivate and protect their "distinctly precious" character. We might even repopulate the dying small places in America by revitalizing what community really means: mutual dependence and attention to the local, in each small place taking our cues from nature.

This vision isn't about putting on your Birkenstocks, sleeping in your tie-dyed yurt, and going back to the land. We're already there. Even in midtown Manhattan, we're on the land. It's about inhabiting every place, fully knowing what the land is there and what it teaches. Living in ways that sustain the ecology of our place. And that includes the people. *Becoming Native* makes it sound so simple: "In the main, all we have to do is provide the context for community to happen and live in a way that will keep it healthy." That means creating a local economy, in the Greek sense of *oikos*, or "household." An economy of interdependence, frugality, and stewardship. Locally based industry that doesn't send its wealth away, reasonable trade relations with other communities, and an absence of consumerism. In the rural world, that makes a farm not a factory but a hearth.

Wes told me the Land was trying to build a sustainable community like that in Matfield Green.

In high school I knew Matfield Green only as a name on the water tower at a rest stop on the Kansas Turnpike. Whenever we traveled out of town by the carload to nine-man-football games, we'd pile out at Matfield Green to load up on Dr. Pepper and chips. The name on the tower made me think of bucolic English greens dotted with grazing sheep. Now I was learning for the first time that Matfield Green, all of fifty-nine miles from Wichita, was not a rest stop but an actual town, current population sixty-nine. The Land had bought and refurbished some of the houses and the hardware store, and had restored the grade school, including putting on a new roof. And now, people attracted by the Wes Jackson magnet had started moving to Matfield to help its community thrive. In the heart of the Flint Hills, too.

The first time I flew from San Francisco back to Kansas, the captain announced that we were flying over the Sierras. I looked down on the range of peaks, where I had hiked trails and swum in lakes and reveled in fields of summer lupines. I didn't know what awaited me in Kansas, but more than I had ever wanted to be in the mountains, I knew I wanted to see the Flint Hills again. An oasis of wild grass, a patch of unplowed prairie hemmed in by the geography of farming, the Flint Hills called to me. When Wes mentioned Matfield Green, I wanted nothing more than to stand in the hills at dusk, my favorite place in Kansas at my favorite time of day.

Girl Scout summers at Camp Wiedeman in the Flint Hills found me and Tara and a hundred other girls canoeing the Fall River, hunting fossils beside the roads, and hiking along the creeks. Each day was filled with swimming classes, crafts, fire-building, whittling, archery, knots, and the boisterous racket of girls. But when the afternoon eased toward evening, the mood of camp shifted. After dinner in the lodge ended and table talk and clinking forks gave way to chores, when the dishes were cleared and the tables washed, we filed outside, all of us quiet, and circled up around the flag pole, our hot, suntanned bodies cooling, bluestem grass bowing across the fields. Standing at attention, we watched the color guard, five girls in red sashes, march smartly up to the pole. While they slowly lowered the flag and folded it into a neat triangle, we held our hands over our hearts, sang "Taps" in three-part harmony, and watched the sun go down.

I finagled an invitation to Matfield Green. When I floated a few hints his direction, Wes said, "You should go and write there for a spell."

So the following summer, I did.

PART THREE

....

Coming Home

[S]eek and learn to recognize who
and what, in the midst of the
inferno, are not inferno, then make
them endure, give them space.

ITALO CALVINO
Invisible Cities

....

CHAPTER NINE

Matfield Green

Clearly, it had been a wet summer. The pastures of the Flint Hills wore a hundred colors of green. I was minutes away from Matfield Green, nestled amid a tangle of creeks and flanked by the south fork of the Cottonwood River. I counted down miles, three, two, one, and then, a loaded semi so hot on my neck, I flew past the three-second stretch of highway that counts as Matfield's Main Street—a handful of houses, small buildings, and a gas station, defunct. It was over before I realized I'd missed it. Slowing down, pulling over, I let the truck pass, then looped back the way I'd come.

Helen Ridder, who managed visitors for the Land, had told me to turn at the Hitchin' Post tavern; and I guessed that the squat red box on the corner must be it. I found Helen just down the street at the Lumberyard, the former hardware store that was now her home, and she showed me where to go.

Home for the next ten days would be a two-story house at the corner of Bocook and Lincoln, with a wooden front porch and a yard full of fruit trees—apple, plum, and pear. Two giant shade trees and a screened-in back porch. White paint, green window trim. The only thing missing was a white picket fence.

I unloaded my city groceries—yogurt, lentils, curry powder, a bag of apples, organic chicken, chocolate bars—and then I started to nest. I put a skillet of moroccan chicken on to simmer and threw prunes in a pot to stew with cinnamon sticks and orange peel. While the pots filled the kitchen with fragrance and steam, I set my laptop up at the kitchen table and watched the cursor blink. I stared out the window into the dark, open mouth of the storm cellar.

Remember when the twister starts to blow and Auntie Em yells and yells for Dorothy, then gives up and goes underground with Uncle Henry? And then Dorothy arrives and pounds on the cellar door, but she can't heave the door open against the wind? Mine was that kind of storm cellar.

But this one had no door, just a deep, black maw in the slope of an earthen mound and crooked wooden steps descending into darkness. Weeds sprouted like crazy hair all over the top, and a ventilation pipe jutted out at an angle. It was tornado season—June; and I thought how I might have to go down there some afternoon or even in the middle of the pitch-black night, groping my way into a gauzy net of spiders. I shuddered.

I switched on the kitchen radio. Farm reports and Christian music. I turned it off. The refrigerator hummed. No TV. A pickup truck rattled down the gravel street toward one of the outlying ranches. I wondered who they were and where they lived. Did they have cows, did they have children, did they get lonely? Did they want to stop for tea?

I kept waiting for something to happen, some turn in the plot. But there was only me and the humming fridge and the bubbling moroccan chicken. And the gaping spider hole out in the yard.

I moved my laptop to the dining room.

Slowly, the days began to roll by. Nobody appeared with a hot pie or a casserole; no one dropped in for a chat. Where was this elusive community reviving the Matfield hum?

I wrote. On a good day, I can write for five hours. Maybe six. In a caffeine-fuelled blitz, maybe seven. That left about twelve hours of daylight to fill. I kept cooking. Wheat berry and black bean salad, lentils and curried rice. Fruit compote. I drove to the Duckworth's in Cottonwood Falls to buy more containers for all the food. And I read. *The Columbia Guide to American Indians of the Great Plains*, Barbara Hurd's *Entering the Stone*. Spider solitaire pulled me into its addictive lair for a while until, finally, I grew so bored with it, quitting was easy.

By day two, whenever I heard crunching gravel, I went to the window, pulled back the curtains, and watched a pickup truck passing, a tractor, a trail of dust. Some days it happened twice. It may have been sheer appetite for company; but more than that, I wanted stories. Anything started to count. Three wasps that snuck into the house then dive-bombed the glass trying to get out. Ants, moths, spiders on their daily rounds. A little black bug as small as the dot on this i traversing a page of *Lewis and Clark on the Great Plains*.

One evening, I sat on the front porch after dinner reading Calvino's *Invisible Cities*. To the great Kublai Khan, Marco Polo recounted tales of the empire's fabulous cities. The gray stone metropolis with blue globes in every room, the spiderweb city, the city on stilts. A city reached by ship or by camel, a city "shrouded in clouds of dirt and grease," "a city with sixty silver domes." I'd read the book three times already, and every city he described, as it always turned out, was Venice. From that one place, Marco Polo had discovered a universe of places.

Back in Matfield Green, the sky went orange in the west. Every half hour, a train whistled through, three blocks away. At the abandoned house across the street, a fat orange tabby settled on his haunches into a caved-in hollow on the porch roof. Watching the weeds for signs of life, he swished his tail, ticktock. The fireflies came out around eight thirty, telegraphing love songs across the lawn. On my side of the street, two lean, stiff-eared rabbits hopped out of the shadows; the cat stiffened and twitched, poised to spring. But then he didn't budge. It seemed he couldn't be bothered with quarry so far away. Birds prattled and complained, and buzzing, flying, hopping things kept smacking into the porch light. I couldn't keep my eye on the page, with so much going on.

The tabby on the collapsing roof started to acknowledge me when he conducted his evening bird count. Every night, we eyed each other for a while. His tail ticktocked. I realized he would never chase anything. I think he knew that I knew.

One afternoon, in the heat of the day, I ventured to the top step of the storm cellar and peered into the dark. It exhaled chilly air. Aaaagh. Like a tomb. Some kind of wooden shelves stood next to the doorway. Clearly, the hole had once sheltered more than spiders. Those shelves had once been loaded with homemade jams and home-canned tomatoes, brown apple butter rich with cinnamon, all in glistening jars. Bins filled with potatoes, onions, and beets. The place was a natural refrigerator. A larder, like mine in the house, filled with a year's worth of meals.

My first four nights were wracked by thunderstorms. The first time, I lay listening to the approaching storm, my feet dangling off the end of the narrow bed. Five in the morning, still dark. I turned off the air conditioner so nothing but storm noise could fill the house. I counted. Five seconds between lightning and thunder boom, five miles away. Three. Two. One. The thumping bass rocked the house, a jagged, branching scar ripped into the dark. The window flashed bright and then dark, flashed and then black. Blacker than the storm shelter doorway. The streetlight had gone out, which meant the electricity had. My hand disappeared in the blackness. Still, I felt safe. My old Kansas knowledge lay sure in my bones; there'd be no tornado. That certain sensation of air pressure, the preternatural stillness that comes just ahead of a twister—I sensed none of them out there in the dark. Just rain pummeling the roof and the orchard trees, thunder rolling a little farther off. My skin tingled with the childhood thrill of riding out a storm in the night.

How many nights had I spent in my parents' basement on an army cot, listening to sirens blaring or to radio reports of tornadoes touching down somewhere to the west or north, to my parents' worried murmuring? Every time had felt like an adventure, the thrill of danger coming near.

After a while—how long?—I woke up in Orchard House to a pale gray sky at the window and a quiet, steady rain, the kind with no plans to move on.

During breakfast Helen called with the weather forecast. More storms tonight. When they came at three—again the flashing sky, the crack, the pitch-black night—I smiled, listened until the storm moved on, then pulled up the covers and slept to the sound of rain. At six I woke again, cranky from city dreams. My bike had been stolen (again), I circled and circled the same city blocks hunting for a parking spot; the people I was supposed to meet were also circling, all of us late, all trapped in the same frustration dream. I had left a meeting—or was it a party?—and stood frozen at the top of a hill so steep that coming down the nearly vertical steps would kill me. I finally found the city's one empty parking space, but so had a dark-haired man. We argued over who found it first. Anger. Shouting. Frustration. Fear.

Matfield is the kind of place, in Wendell Berry's words,

> where thought
> can take its shape
> as quietly in the mind
> as water in a pitcher.

I began to feel content with my daily dramas. The city rhythms thrumming in my veins began to fade, and a different pulse measured out my days. Most of the day, I pondered, gazed out the window. The pages started coming. The last night of storms, during another blackout, at two in the morning, a lightning bug crawled up the wall. I watched its tiny bulb blink here and then there, the flashes marking his progress like moving punctuation.

During the day, I walked. I learned to go out early or late to avoid the afternoon swelter. One morning, I walked out past the Cottonwood River, which was gushing and muddy from the rain. Topsoil down the drain. Strips of wild prairie rioted along the road—lavender milkweed and thistle, clouds of daisy fleabane, waist-high Indian and bluestem grasses, spiky blue vervain. I had read somewhere that 10 million insects live on every acre of prairie. When the sun came out, I believed it. As though someone had flipped a switch, thousands of inch-long grasshoppers began flicking themselves about. Hundreds of cream-colored butterflies came floating, drifting, and wavering in columns, like torn bits of onionskin paper. I tried to photograph a few sunning themselves on the orange-blossomed butterfly milkweed, opening and closing their gold-dusted prayer-book wings. But they wouldn't sit still. They kept fluttering and alighting, dozens on my arm, on the camera lens, my knee. One sat on the back of my hand and unfurled its long, curling drinking straw of a tongue as if to sip from my knuckle.

West of town, through a tunnel under the railroad grade, the road followed the contours of the hills, curving in a wide arc and riding the ridge. I liked to stand up there and drink in the view. In a big Crayola box of greens, low hills, one curving into the next, ran all the way to the horizon. Swaths of darker green, the swelling of trees, spread along the creases and creek beds. Across the pastures bloomed sprays of butterfly milkweed and the last of the season's blue wild indigo. Poison ivy and wild squash sprawled in the ditches.

My first walk out that direction, a herd of cows came running. They stopped halfway across the field and stared. They looked like paper cutouts against the green. Soon, I could tell one cow from another. I started conversing with a black-and-white one that always ran to the fence. She wore a big, yellow plastic tag in her ear. Number eighty-seven. I remarked to her about the weather, the wildflowers, passed the time with pleasantries. She seemed attentive, twitching her black, velveteen ear.

The first time I came back to Kansas, that time in October, I'd come to the Flint Hills to the Tallgrass Prairie National Preserve near Strong City, one of the last remaining stands of original tallgrass prairie. The day was cold and wet, the sky gray, the parking lot empty. I hiked in the quiet, every step swishing the wet grass, my breath puffing out a vapor trail. The dampness quickly soaked the legs of my jeans and seeped into my tennis shoes. The grass, all stems and stalks and tattered seed pods, had been stripped of its summer green.

When the trail climbed a low rise, I struggled up the slippery path, my breath puffing faster and louder, until finally I reached the top. The hills rolled away, yellow and brown, all the way to the low horizon. From where I stood, a little footpath, as thin as a ribbon, wound down the side of the hill and scrambled up another, where it reached the door of a little stone one-room schoolhouse. The sky hung low and met the hills on the far side. Catching my breath, I caught back tears and said aloud to no one, whoever thinks Kansas isn't beautiful has never been here.

Here was the land of summer camp, my "remembered earth," the one that Momaday writes of and that, back in San Francisco, I thought I'd never had. This place had taught me names like "daisy fleabane" and "Queen Anne's lace" and "meadowlark." Its seasons lay like a memory on my skin, the cold spring rain, the summer heat, the low-autumn sun. The bright fierceness of a blizzard, the bite of winter wind.

Now atop the ridge outside Matfield Green, I knew that I, a child of Kansas, had imprinted on this land, been shaped by its subtleties and sweep, so that in coming here, I found myself at home. A sweet, familiar breeze cooled my arms and set the grasses waving. It stirred the cottonwoods by a pasture gate, rattling their soft leaves like fine sand spilling on a hardwood floor. Like small rain.

Over dinner with Helen at the Lumberyard, I told her about the cow. Without so much as a raised eyebrow, she said she liked to drive out into the hills, park in the middle of some green place, and sing to the cows, loud and off-key. They like human company, she said, and they like music. Since Helen likes to sing, it works out.

Helen is a nun; but if your concepts of nuns run to habits and hushed tones or rulers on knuckles, you'd never be able to tell.

She belongs to the Adorers of the Blood of Christ, but in Matfield Green she lived alone. People don't know anything about nuns, she said, you can be in an order and live alone. She had come there to be closer to nature. It was her spiritual work. She'd grown up in Goddard, not far from Matfield, although between growing up and coming back, she had traveled. A few years back, she went to Rome for a spiritual retreat, and she and her sister nuns had two extra weeks to spend. Everyone but Helen wanted to go to the Marian shrine in Medjugorje. If she wanted to pray to Mary, Helen figured, she could pray to Mary anywhere. So while the other nuns lit candles and prayed in Bosnia and Herzegovina, Helen strolled the Uffizi in Florence.

In the sixties, when many young women left the order, Helen stayed. She had wondered for years who was doing God's work— those who had left or those who hadn't. She finally decided they all were. And though Helen stayed, she doesn't follow blindly. She has no patience, she said, with the hierarchy of the church or with most priests, who come out of seminary "thinking they're God on a platter."

After dinner she showed me around the school. The hallways smelled of oiled oak floors and chalk. The library, which now belongs to the town, contained novels, textbooks, and field guides to the prairie. In one classroom a row of bunk beds stood against the tall windows—a dorm for the Land Institute brainstorming conclaves they call "Matfield Greens." The industrial-sized kitchen and dining room turned the school into an all-purpose community hub. Portraits of everyone living in Matfield Green in 1994 lined the hall outside the principal's office, along with students' photographs: cows in golden late-summer pastures, high-tension wires strung across a ridge, a prairie fire burning its ragged black line across a field.

Helen told me about a woman who had grown up in Matfield and still lived there. Like several folks in town, she was in her nineties. She had gone to this school, Helen marveled, and played on the women's basketball team. And would you know that seventy-five years ago this little town with its little school had a sports program so advanced that women played full-court basketball? In bloomers, she added, but they played. In Helen's hometown, girls were thought too weak for full-court, so Helen had had to play half-court ball. Of course, after school the girls would be out there throwing hay bales, right alongside their brothers. She still heated up, remembering it.

Afterward, we walked up the street and poked around the empty house, the one with the porch-roof cat. I hadn't dared go in, but Helen strode right through the weeds, stepped across some broken boards, and into the living room. The people had simply walked away, leaving a rocking chair, a sewing machine, a pair of shoes. They had cut the fabric right off the windows in the back bedroom, leaving six inches of ragged blue fabric dangling from the rings. I started to assess. Six rooms, hardwood floors, a decent-sized kitchen, and a back sun porch. I would rip out the bad seventies additions in the front room, shag carpet and sprayed acoustic ceiling with sparkles. Plant a vegetable garden and fruit trees out back. Flower beds. Strawberries. Solar panels. Rain barrels.

"You could buy it, fix it up," Helen suggested. "It's so cheap."

Hmmm. For $50,000 I could both buy and renovate the house. In San Francisco $50,000 wouldn't even buy a doghouse. Here, I could have my dacha, a garden, evenings on the front porch, and a prairie just up the road. I could rent the house to the Land Institute when I wasn't around, move in for two months every summer, for a year every sabbatical. Of course, reason intruded—I would see my house only once or twice a year and have to travel halfway across the continent to get there. My newly acquired husband would have to be wooed to the cause. He had happily left his childhood state of Illinois and looked back without longing, but I figured he just hadn't yet had his epiphany about the virtues of rural life. I told Helen I would think about it.

When she headed back to the Lumberyard, the sun still hovered above the horizon and something sweet—honeysuckle?—floated on the air. Birds fussed in the orchard trees, and the crickets tuned up for the coming dark.

After days of talking only to cows and to Helen, I entered Matfield society and soaked it up like a thirsty plant. During one of my morning walks, Ron Armstrong pulled up beside me in an ancient Olds station wagon. He said that Helen had sent him, and would I like to see the old railroad bunkhouse? A mile or so out of town, the bunkhouse had provided unheated, uninsulated, overcrowded housing for generations of rail workers. It had fallen into disuse when the railroads did; but Bill McBride, a Chicago architect, was bringing it back to life. He was to retire in a year, and he and his wife Julia planned on moving in.

Ron and I wandered the four rooms, stepping over nails and boards. The bunkhouse had a new underfloor heating system, insulation, and new doors and windows. Bare studs waited for walls.

As I write this in the fall of 2006, Bill and Julia have now planted a garden inside the old corral, where cattle waited to be herded onto the train. They're growing watermelon, cantaloupe, green beans, garlic, tomatoes, and chard. They're raising a barn and a bigger house, and they host an annual pig roast. Julia's blog reports that this year 150 people came, everyone bringing a covered dish. A farmer they didn't even know donated a pig.

Back in Matfield, Ron and I dropped in on Emily Hunter. Tall, red haired, and freckled, Emily had left Boulder ten years earlier for Matfield Green. Now she ran the Living Education Project, teaching children about where they live—its seasons, soils, grasses, fauna, how the prairie sends down roots. When she first came, she'd bought a big house up on the highway and had it moved to her six-acre lot where North Madden curves into Brandley, a quarter mile north of Orchard House. She had knocked out most of the ceiling, exposing the rafters and leaving two sleeping lofts up under the eaves. Giant ceiling fans from a dismantled school turned slowly in the summer air. In her backyard a neighbor was building Emily a duplex chicken coop, one side for chickens, the other for guinea hens. Emily hoped they would help with the grasshoppers, which were devouring her herb garden. Hoppers eat flower petals right down to the stem, she told me, and in dry summers without much greenery, they'll even chew up the window screens.

That night, Matfield Green's new people gathered at Emily's for dinner. Helen came, along with Kathy and Phil, who lived in the yellow Victorian on Reed, their yard full of daylilies. Bill McBride showed up with his partner, in town to check on the bunkhouse; they'd be showing it to a "gang of railroad nuts" in the morning. Ron and his wife Barb, who had traveled the world but preferred the Flint Hills, brought locally grown green beans. They also brought Thelma, who'd lived her ninety-one years in Matfield Green.

Afraid of how the town might change, Matfield's old-timers didn't quite trust the new folks for a while; but they've come to a peaceful accord. Thelma, a tiny woman, wore little black cowboy boots and purple pants, a reddish brown wig and crooked painted-on eyebrows. She had just returned from visiting her son in Virginia. He sends her a ticket every year.

"I don't want to go," she said in her nasal Kansas twang, "but he sends me that durn ticket and I have to. He wants to give me experiences I wouldn't get otherwise. It was a good experience. But I wasn't goin' in that water. I took off my shoes and waded at the edge, and a big ole wave, she came right up to my knees. I'm scared of water that deep. And it was cold as ice. I'm from the country, you know. Never did see the ocean before. It was a good experience."

While Thelma told her story, Barb snapped beans and tossed them in a pot. We sat down to pasta, spinach salad, and green beans, and to rich political talk. The new people were all progressive or populist, suspicious of Republicans, in favor of social spending, and hard on big money. Thelma listened, nodding her head and peppering the conversation with an occasional "you're durn right."

Emily had just come from Cottonwood Falls, fifteen miles north, where the board of the new Symphony on the Prairie had just convened. They'd planned an annual summer concert to be held in different ranchers' fields with a temporary stage and folding chairs. The whole thing would spring up like a mushroom and then disappear, fading in the next morning's sun. The grass would rebound, and cattle retake the field. The goal was to create culture and community that honored the land, keeping things not provincial but local.

I imagined my life there. While I fixed up my house, I would help with the symphony, walk out in the hills, share dinner with people who chose this place because they love it. And because they—who have lived in Boulder and Yellowstone and countries abroad—want to live simply, with the prairie and one another. I wanted to be there, too.

I like to think my dreams of living in Matfield arose because Matfield Green, or the idea of it, brought together all of the things I had missed growing up in Kansas. A place where I could stay and belong in a community. And because it was planted on the prairie, in tune with its seasons and its tangled roots, I could plant myself as I never had been, weave my life into the cycles of the year, and dwell in the landscape that had shaped my heart.

Or was this all nothing more than the fantasies of a traveler, like my young backpacker's dream of living on the beach in Greece? Or my summer scholar's dream of living in that London flat only a good, brisk walk from the British Library? Or maybe it was nothing more than a desire for safety, an escape from the threat of cancer, shelter from the storm.

In my second morning in Matfield, I sat at the dining room table, glanced at the Kansas map, and decided to write about cancer. Two years and more had passed since those watershed months—diagnosis, surgery, chemo, radiation, and my first trip back to Kansas. Kansas and cancer, two unlike things linked by sequence, first this, then that. Enough time had passed to write about both. First this, then that. But lying there together, notes about cancer, maps of Kansas, they seemed to suggest a deeper entwining.

The body, I thought, is a place made strange by disease. First the jolt of finding a lump, then the bigger shock of bad news. The body's suddenly traitorous fallibility. The technologies of treatment that made it stranger still.

Somewhere in the bowels of the hospital, I am gowned and capped, lying on the table, waiting for my surgeon, Dr. Silvey. It seems too prosaic a place for what's about to happen, an empty, cavernous room with a linoleum floor, like in anyone's kitchen, and white cabinets on the wall. I am here for a sentinel node procedure. Sentinel lymph nodes, I've learned, stand at the gates of my lymph system; and if my cancer has traveled beyond the tumor, the sentinels will have soaked it up first. Dr. Silvey is coming to inject the radioactive tracer that will help map where things have gone. The blue dye will make the nodes easy to find when he goes to cut them out in the afternoon.

A nurse enters and draws the pale blue curtains around me, creating a smaller, cotton-swathed room, a more intimate place for me and my nodes. On the steel table next to me, she lays out syringes, tears open paper-wrapped cotton squares, and lines up vials and latex gloves. As though her hands have nothing to do with her, they continue to work while she talks about the beautiful, clear blue day outside. She squeezes my hand and says, "you're going to be fine," then whisks away on her quiet, white-soled shoes.

I start to meditate, eyes closed, and feel my body give way to the rhythm of my breath. When Dr. Silvey appears in green surgical garb and asks me how I'm doing, I feel suddenly shy. It's like a first date with the boy I've sat next to in calculus class for weeks—suddenly, we find ourselves alone at the Dairy Queen. Everything seems new; he seems new. We've changed our costumes, his white lab coat for green scrubs, my usual paper blue gown for this drab, drapey cotton one with stripes. Of course, he's perfectly at home. I'm the stranger here. His eyes shine with confident delight, like the bright schoolboy's who has been asked to solve the very hard math problem. I tell him I'm ready, let's go.

He holds a syringe up to the light, taps out the bubbles, then tilts the needle toward my breast. This first needle will numb the tissue, preparing it for the larger needles filled with blue dye. At last, I think, I'm in it. Each thing will happen now in turn: biopsy, surgery, chemo, radiation. It's February. I'll be done by September. I've started, I can finish, and I feel glad. I focus on the ceiling, breathing in and breathing out, and feel the tiny sting of the needle; but I breathe, simply letting it come. It quickly passes, and Dr. Silvey leaves to let the numbing begin.

Like any place, like Kansas, the body plays many roles, can mean many things. I think of the skinned knees and chicken pox and appetites of childhood—those lessons of fragility and resiliency and the body's capacity for pain, hunger, yearning, pleasure, and sheer kinetic joy. I remember how my young woman's body swelled in pregnancy, the skin taut across my belly; how it sweated and writhed in giving birth; how it has reveled in the pleasures of sex; and how it now harbors the multiplying madness of a tumor. The landscape of my body wears its history in memories and scars, and now its meanings seem permanently changed.

In the pamphlet *A Woman's Guide*, which the surgeon's nurse had given me, the woman in the diagrams has had her head cut off above the lips and her body, below the navel. She has no arms below the elbow. She is her breasts alone. My own breast has come to seem an alien thing, a parasite, an anarchic appendage, a danger. My focus, my attention, my energy, my knowing—all focus on that one breast, like the woman in the pamphlet. It has become the only body that matters. Today the lump, at least, will be gone.

"Now, this will hurt," Dr. Silvey says. He has appeared from somewhere and filled another syringe. I take a deep breath and feel a dull stab, then a burn, like a hot coat-hanger wire searing into the flesh. Dr. Silvey pulls and pushes the needle, slowly releasing dye, massaging it into the tissue. I am aware of the pain, but still I focus on my breath. The second needle, another jab, another hot wire. My concentration begins to slip. I feel the pull of pain, the desire to clench my mind around it like a fist. I struggle to focus, breathe. Then it happens a third time. Dull stab, hot wire. A little fountain of cobalt blue spurts from my nipple. I catch my breath. Dr. Silvey marvels: "Wow. I must have hit a milk duct. That's a first." My tears well up, he wipes away the little blue puddle.

During the years I was nursing, I watched each baby suck until she fell asleep, sweaty cheek against my breast, warm milk pooling up in the corner of her mouth, then pulled the nipple away and watched her lips kissing the air, dreaming her sweet milk dreams. Such days of intense physicality, of my body feeding another, skin on skin. Now my breast is aflame and throbbing. My daughters, the milk-fed babies now grown, are waiting in Austin and in Oregon to hear how this day goes. As the fourth needle goes in, tears of pity for my wounded breast leak out the corner of my eye.

Three hours later, I stand behind a screen and the gamma counter spits out its picture of my radioactive self. Dr. Silvey holds up the film to explain. The image is supposed to map my body, but no bodily outline appears, no recognizable form as there would be with an x-ray, a ghostly torso lying over the bones. Instead, it's a fireworks display, a spray of gold sparkles on black. The angry cluster of sparks marks my tumor, and thin trails like ant tracks lead to the two smaller clumps that Dr. Silvey says are my sentinel nodes. The cancer, it seems, has traveled the ant trails. More than anything else, the film looks like the view from a plane at night, the dense orange brightness of the city unraveling at the edges, unspooling long threads of light out into the darkness, where they end in the tangled constellation of a village or the lone starry twinkle of a farm. My radiant body, the body electric, a city from the sky at night. But not even the distance between the sparkly clusters matches the size of my body. I don't recognize myself.

A disease like cancer strips the body of its imagined immortality, and also of its metaphors. The maternal breast, the sexual breast— and during baldness-inducing chemo, the femininity of hair—the cultural meanings of the female body. Estranged from our preconceptions, the diseased body becomes what it is: time bound, mammalian, finite, flesh. And then comes the question, who am I now? And how then do I live?

Disease, like any other symptom of mortality, also foretells our last estrangement from the body, that ultimate unmooring when we are stripped of all our metaphors and simply slip away. So maybe that was the connection between the Kansas map and the cancer notes on the table in Matfield Green. For death bears the same design as all those losses that had sent me back to Kansas in the first place: my childhood houses, my childhood schools, my father, my parents, and more recently, P and the Victorian house. Perhaps my original question, what does Kansas have to do with me? was really, what shall I do, then, with my temporal life? Perhaps all those journeys back, while I learned Kansas more deeply, while I explored Pawnee ruins, while I toured the Land Institute, were ways of answering the ultimate question: how do I live deeply in the place I find myself, in the life that is, knowing how short its duration?

In Kansas and in meditation, I was learning how to answer the questions. Seated on my cushion, I had learned the dwelling of close attention: on the breath, on the heart, on what arises and passes away. And from the Pawnees and the Land, I had learned about deep dwelling in community and in the breath and rhythms of the earth. I was learning to know and dwell deeply in things as they are.

After dinner at Emily's, I walked back to Orchard House at eleven, crickets singing, stars out. I was alert, my city reflexes attuned to anything that might signal trouble. But there was no trouble, no one else around. Just crickets and small animals shuttling in the grass. The fat tom sauntered across the road and nodded, gave me a languid, two-eyed wink.

In *Invisible Cities*, Marco Polo tells a story of the city Cecilia. There, he meets a herdsman who says that to him all cities look the same. "They are places without leaves, separating one pasture from another, and where the goats are frightened at street corners and scatter." Marco Polo admits that he, on the other hand, can only distinguish cities and not the green spaces in between. "In uninhabited places each stone and each clump of grass mingles, in my eyes, with every other stone and clump."

Many years pass and Polo finds himself in another city, not quite sure of its name. "Walking among rows of identical houses," he admits he is lost. So he asks a passerby where he is, and the fellow turns out to be the goatherd from years before. The man tells Polo that he is in Cecilia. He and his goats, he laments, "have been wandering its streets . . . for an age and cannot find [their] way out." Marco Polo is astonished, for he had entered a city far away from Cecilia and had "gone on, deeper and deeper into its streets" without leaving it. How, he asks the goatherd, had he ended up in Cecilia? The goatherd explains, "The places have all mingled. . . . Cecilia is everywhere. Here, once upon a time, there must have been the Meadow of the Low Sage. My goats recognize the grass on the traffic island."

This time when I read about Cecilia, my loyalties shifted. For me, a lover of cities, the tale had become a parable of Matfield Green, of all the Matfield Greens that had been made irrelevant. Cecilia is everywhere. The city has swallowed up the prairie. Physically in its expansiveness, economically in its voraciousness. The spaces in between, whether "seas, or fields of rye, larch forests or swamps," don't matter.

Did we city people think of the meadow when we saw that tuft of grass sprouting on a traffic island? Did we think of the farm when we ate our baby greens? Did we notice the absence of the green world in the way we live and the stories we tell of our lives? This was the world I wanted to attend to, to notice, to meditate on. To live in.

On my last night in Matfield, I felt restless. I had read all the books I'd brought, written plenty of pages, eaten most of the food in my larder. I needed to be outdoors. Ten minutes outside of Matfield, I pulled off the road and waited for sunset. The western sky had filled with clouds, white billows swelling. The sun had already slipped behind them, making the top edge glow as if to say, come lie down here and rest. Along the horizon the clouds had turned the dusky blue of a concord grape, while at the center a chink let the light stream through. The gap slowly widened, opening like a curtain, until the sun shone luminous and whole and then began to sink behind the lip of another cloud. Wispy horsetails drifted across. The light shifted and the sun—suspended, pulsing—shimmered in a crystalline cave, its radiance dampened by the chill. Then the light dimmed, the clouds grew more somber, and the entire western sky became a sea shore after a storm—boulders and rocks, water splashing and surging, sun glinting off the rippling shoals. For more than a minute the image stayed, glittering water, breaking waves. Gradually the sea darkened into sky, the clouds brightened again like alabaster, and then went slowly dark. The entire cloud bank became a purple mass, and a diaphanous sash floated across. Sailing above the mass, a small fleet of nimbus clouds suddenly switched on, peach and orange and pink, buoyant on the sun's last rays. They floated then faded, and all the clouds, cumulous and nimbus, large and small, took on the colors of dark. Their hulking silhouette lay flat against a sky newly filled with stars.

None of this happened in silence. The prairies are alive at dusk, noisier at sunset than at any other hour. While the drama of the sun and clouds unfolded from opening theme to final chord, the prairie birds were settling in. Chattering, one note, two notes, trilling, the tender lament of the mourning dove, the high-pitched whistle of the scissortails swooping in their orbits over the grass. For the entire hour it took the sun to set, a syncopated racket filled the air, the clangor and gong of call-and-response, hoot, challenge, complaint. A cow came in on the bass line. The moment the sky went dark, they stopped. The prairie settled into silence. A single trill from a mead-owlark sailed out across the grass, and then the world was still.

The next morning, my last one in Matfield, I was packing when someone knocked on the door. My neighbor Victor. I'd met Victor on one of my morning walks. He had been sitting on the abutment by the river, relaxing in his baggy blue jeans and suspenders, his white shirt sprinkled with pale blue chevrons. He looked at me through thick, bottle-glass lenses then looked back down at the river. He gestured with his walking stick. "Hasn't rained this much in years," he said. "It's what makes everything so green." He had a cleft palate and I was from the city, but we understood each other pretty well. He lived in Matfield Green, he said, always had, on the corner just up from Orchard House. His was the brick house with the windmill in the yard.

Victor had been in Matfield long enough to know who had lived in every empty house or vacant lot and where every family had gone. When I opened the door, he said he'd heard I was writing a book about Kansas, and did I want to see his picture of Matfield Green? He thought it might be something to see. I said I'd love to, so he went home to fetch it.

He came back carrying a large, framed black-and-white aerial shot taken before the railroad came through in 1923. Victor peered through his thick glasses and, with a blunt finger, pointed out various features. "Here's the church," he said, jabbing at the glass, "and the cemetery, and there's the one house on the highway you can still see." The town had always been small, but in the photo it was a whole town, with more than one hardware store, a post office, a general store, and houses on every lot. "There's Orchard House," he pointed out, "there's the orchard. And there's the storm cellar." There it was, a low mound in the side yard. I'd been feeling friendly toward the storm cellar, and I liked seeing it in the photo.

For thirty years, Victor had driven to Wichita to work at Boeing; but having grown up in Matfield, he had always wanted to stay. Now retired, a little past eighty, he walked to the creek every morning and sat on his porch in the late afternoon, the windmill in his yard creaking in the breeze. I could think of nothing lovelier at the moment than that slow, steady cadence of days.

"This here," Victor said, "is where they put in the railroad. You can see they were already building the grade." He touched his finger to the glass. And just as it had every time he'd pointed out a building or a house or the cemetery, his finger went wide of the mark, landing on the sky or a tree or the road. I realized that, even with his thick lenses, Victor couldn't really see. It hardly mattered; he knew Matfield Green by heart.

When a place lives in you beyond the limits of the senses, when its many maps are laid on your heart, maybe that's when you really belong to it. When it belongs to you. When you know its people and its rivers and its seasons and the stories that mark the land. When one little place, like Marco Polo's Venice, can give you a world of stories. It can be enough.

When Victor took his photo home, I swept twigs from the porch and carried my suitcase to the car. The tom watched from across the street. I longed for that house. But now that I was leaving, that other world began to speak, too. City of bridges, city of streetcars, city of movies, city of Oz. I longed for it, too, even while I felt the tug of wanting to stay. Of needing more than the grass on a traffic island. When I wrote my story, I'd want the green places, too.

As I drove away, the sycamores soughed and sighed, and out beyond the railroad tracks, along the curving ridge, the tall grass and the butterflies and the wildflowers and the wind all sang to me, come away.

Coda, 2008

Four years have passed since my Matfield idyll, and still, I haven't moved there.

I moved to L.A.

I sit on my balcony some afternoons—cut off from views by a ficus hedge—and visit other places in my mind's eye. Bean There Café on a foggy San Francisco morning, with steam jetting from the espresso machine, a neighbor's golden retriever outside lapping water from a metal bowl. Sand Creek in Colorado, where wind moves through the grass. China Garden in Goodland, two beige houses in Hays. The rushing headwaters of the Arkansas in the Rockies, its wide, slow arc through Wichita. Spring pastures blooming in the Flint Hills.

But the mind's eye is not the body's knowing. Luckily, I still work in San Francisco. Unluckily for someone allergic to moving, I commute, shuttling between this sprawling world where sunshine's the only weather, a place indifferent to the body's scale of things, and a cool, moody city I have measured by the length of my stride. When the school season is on, I still grade papers in Bean There, chat with my neighbors, bike through Golden Gate Park to the beach.

Sometimes I still slip across the border and head for Kansas. I feel connected there. And whole.

On my first night in L.A. after the movers had gone, I sat on the floor amid the boxes, sobbing as usual. As usual, too, I rallied, though I am still feeling my way. The last time I flew back to California from

Kansas, my brain filled with prairie twilight, prairie wind, we came in low over the hundred-mile square of the electrified L.A. grid. Red and white rivers of car lights streamed across the terrain; the Los Angeles River, poisoned by runoff, lay entombed in concrete. Despondent, I thought, this cannot last. If we are to survive, the future has to lie back there in the roots of the prairie. In its lessons of sustainability, community, and earth.

I could despair about making a place for myself here. I sometimes do. But I no longer dream of going home to Kansas. My work is here, becoming native to the place where I find myself. Finding and nurturing the green world inside my city life. Letting the place teach me. Peeling back the layered accretions of history, culture, and migration; gathering those stories as I go. Stripping away the myths. The stereotypes. The hype. I can join the Friends of the Los Angeles River, ride the West Coast fault lines of tectonic bump and grind. Learn what geology, weather, and soil can tell me.

A mile north of my West Hollywood apartment, in Runyon Canyon, I am learning to recognize yarrow, black sage, and sticky monkeyflower. The plants still green in August, the ones that bloom in spring, the ones that thrive without sprinklers or the army of gardeners who manicure the promised land. Every Monday, I buy local organic romaine and oranges from the West Hollywood farmers' market. I chat with Mr. Ha about his apple orchards and with the honey lady about her bees. And when I can, I do the L.A. unheard-of. I walk. When I can't do that, I hop on public transit. I've sold my car.

It's not enough, not nearly. But in a city alien to a deep sense of place, a city that violates nature's limits, it's what I can do. As Wes Jackson says, if we have to walk the talk, we'll never get there.

In the meantime, until we get there, I'll continue with my new life in microscale farming. In San Francisco I've snagged a plot in the community garden on my campus. Lettuce, arugula, and chard crowd my window boxes at home; and my annual tomato plantation enjoyed a bumper first year. Right there beneath the bay windows of my third-floor Edwardian flat, I planted the seeds I'd saved from an heirloom tomato I bought ($4.99 a pound). Like a host of little miracles, they sprang up into sixty little plants that have now made their way in the world. One's growing on a friend's balcony in Berkeley; two, on a landing in the South Bay. Twenty-five found a home in the campus garden, and a dozen or so went to a friend's organic farm farther north. My three best plants came home to L.A. Sprawling like jungle vines and heavy with fruit, they don't seem to mind growing in pots on the sunny balcony across from my neighbors' door. Neighbors whom I'd never met until the tomato plants arrived, and who happily share their sun in exchange for homegrown Brandywines. The neighbors next to them recently put out their own pots of tomatoes and basil and peppers. And so community grows.

I came to L.A. by following my filmmaker-husband Frederick. It's an experiment, to see if his work needs Hollywood soil to thrive. The ironies seem rich, me on the move again in support of an artist's dreams. But this artist is not my father. Though I haven't yet convinced him to come outside and get some garden dirt under his nails, still he is wise, grounded in the practice of awareness and the nature of change.

Hollywood, where the circle meets itself, the ouroboros catches its tail. My father's beginning, his rainbow's end. Whenever I pass the MGM lot, I think of my grandfather Leon arriving for a day of filming *A Day at the Races*. I think of the Hollywood Canteen and my father when I walk past Hollywood High. At sixteen, raging at the principal, he stormed out of school and never went back. On my morning walks, whenever I pass a little clapboard house from the thirties, I wonder if he might have walked or ridden his bike past, or lived in a house just like it. One of these days, I might take my uncle Carl's list of seventeen addresses and visit one of my father's houses. If this restless city, ever new, hasn't torn it down.

Like L.A., San Francisco keeps drawing dreamers west. A month ago, as the semester was winding down, I sat in the Haight to Wash

Laundromat waiting for the dryers to stop sucking up my quarters and the towels to finally dry. The Bay to Breakers race had ended, and contestants were pouring back into the neighborhood, runners in face paint and togas and tutus shouting and laughing, spilling over the sidewalks, dancing in the street. A fleet of young women in dragonfly wings sailed, giggling, by. A man in a clown car was driving up and down the sidewalk broadcasting a tinkly ice-cream-truck tune; and an older man passing by on his jaunty way to somewhere poked his head in the open Laundromat door and, looking right at me, reeled off a romantic rap stanza or two, and then without comment continued on his way.

The young man who had quietly been folding his laundry near the window turned to me, wide-eyed. "Is it always like this here?"

"Pretty much," I told him. Clearly, he was new in these parts. I explained about the foot race. "Where'd you move from?"

"Troy, Kansas."

Kansas! When I told him I'd come from there, too, his shy face broke into a smile. We talked for a while about where we'd grown up, shared our common landscape. I wondered how growing up in a small farming town had been for such a slight, pale, and gentle boy. I told him he'd get used to San Francisco, and he looked forward to it. He said he'd been saving up to move here since he was thirteen. Another escapee to the Emerald City. I told him I hoped he wouldn't leave what was good about Kansas behind.

And so the circle comes round.

Until finishing these last pages, I had hoped to close another circle. For years, I had remembered visiting my first sister Tara's grave in Forest Lawn in Glendale, L.A.'s cemetery to the stars. At this point in my coda, I foresaw visiting her grave. But then I made the mistake of calling Forest Lawn. No record of her there.

As it turns out, she's buried in Des Moines. As my sisters reminded me, we didn't go to the graveyard after Disneyland and Knott's Berry Farm, as I was sure we had, but during a family trip back to Iowa.

I'd forgotten. I suppose it's because my emotional compass—

attracted by our family trips to California and my father's hold on my heart—has long been pointed west. And I suppose I had wanted the symmetry of burying that baby in the place I'd finally landed.

How fitting that I should be so wrong about where my sister died, where my parents grieved, where they left her behind. Disconnection from place makes us lose more than our bearings.

In February of 2006 my cancer came out of remission and took up residence in my bones. More likely than not, it will one day do me in.

Living with a life-threatening disease requires wisely choosing our metaphors. Some cancer patients say we're at war with an enemy within. Obituaries read, "died after a long battle." Or as I once imagined, cancer is a foreign country. Once in a while, a healthy person will ask what it's like to live with the threat of such a dark cloud, or with that sword of Damocles they see dangling above my head. Others suspect that all my actions must be marked or motivated by the chill of not knowing how much time is left. How afraid I must be. But cancer, whatever else it may be, is also a Rorschach test, a screen on which others project their own fears of mortality, test out their own metaphors. If they would be afraid, I must be. If they would feel the chill of shortening days, I must wear a sweater.

I choose other metaphors. Fear, of course, has its moments in my days. When it arises, I greet it like a familiar. Hello, I say, there you are. But fear lives on future time, and I choose not to live there. I breathe and let it go. Living with cancer for me is not fighting a battle, or being pursued by a cloud, or feeling the chill air of the tomb on my neck. It is not the house I live in. Cancer, like any fate given to anyone might be, is simply the road I walk. And death is like the storm cellar in the yard at Orchard House. I can fear the darkness and spiders inside, or I can fill it with the fruits of the earth. Jars and roots and signs of life.

Or death may be like Jim Burden imagines it when he lays himself down in the tall grass, becoming "part of something entire . . . dissolved into something complete and great." His vision is the vision of the Buddha's enlightenment, to be, as I was in my own tallgrass dream, dissolved into something complete and great, beyond self, beyond body, beyond ego, beyond time.

In the meantime, I'll keep breathing, in, out. Meditating on the raisin, tasting the present, not leaping too far ahead. It's amazing what a little tomato plantation can do, growing, fruiting, dying, leaving seeds for next year like a gift. More firmly woven in to that web that makes place, and life, both ephemeral and enduring—I have little trouble, most of the time, letting the rest go.

Acknowledgments

Like all books, this one flows from a thousand sources, through a hundred guiding hands. I am grateful.

In the beginning: Jane Anne Staw read and nurtured my first stuttering starts. So did my fellow Wednesday writers, David Holler and Darrell Schramm. Darrell also makes a mean apple pancake and understands loving the High Plains. Vijiya Nagarajan introduced me to helpers and friends, and Lee Swenson set my course for Wes Jackson's back yard, which turned out to be exactly where I needed to go.

Along the way: Phillip Lopate allowed a stranger to toss an ungainly draft over his transom and responded with kind words. Dawn Marano, the kind of editor every writer deserves, offered the painful advice: restructure. She was right. Elizabeth Dodd has been a keen and exacting reader who pushed in knowing directions, and Bob Root cheered me on. Hilda Raz, Barbara Hurd, and Mike Chorost advised and encouraged in just the right ways. Doug Powell, Kate Brady, and Aaron Shurin still do.

On the road: I thank the curators and docents at the Denver Museum of Colorado History, the Museum of Western Colorado, the Ute Museum in Montrose, the Pawnee Village Museum in Republic, the Kansas State Historical Museum in Topeka, the Brown-Adair cabin in Osawatomie, the Quivira Museum in Lyons, the Independence Historical Museum, and the Brown v. Board of

Education Museum. I especially thank Sally Johnson at the Raymer Red Barn Museum in Lindsborg, David Branda and Carol Baum at the Sherman County Historical Society, Evelyn Splattsoesser at the Carnegie Library Arts Center in Goodland, and Mrs. Hesston at the Goodland Museum.

Thanks, too, to Don Moore in Nicodemus, for his time and stories during homecoming weekend. And to Denise Low, professor at Haskell Indian Nations University and former poet laureate of Kansas, for her generosity and her work.

I also thank the people now living in or near my family's former homes who suffered my curiosity and took me in, especially Colleen and Tom Heard in Grand Junction, Leslie Gray in Colorado Springs, Bill Nichols in Wichita, and Anna Jean Ford in Hays.

In thanking Wes Jackson, I add my name to a very long list of debtors. Thank you, Wes, for the ride on the merry-go-round and for the gift of time at Matfield Green. In that little corner of the Flint Hills, Helen, Ron, Barb, and Emily showed me what is possible. Melinda Stone, back in San Francisco, shared my joy in digging in the dirt.

While writing: Gifts of time and space came from benefactors and friends. I thank Edward Albee for time at the Barn and John and Nell Able for the pear-orchard summer. Ron Biela sheltered me at the start of my first two trips to Kansas and has kept up a remarkable epistolary conversation now for nigh on thirty years. I also thank Charla, whose love of art and decades of friendship have been the best kind of refuge.

The University of San Francisco has unblinkingly supported me in this detour from what I was supposed to be doing. The NEH chair gave me a running start and the funds to create a collaborative, campus-wide year devoted to place. Thank you to the USF faculty and staff who imagined, wrote, painted, sculpted, filmed, and thought out loud about place and who helped me think my own thoughts more clearly. Faculty-development grants funded my trips back to Kansas, even when one trip turned into four. The same funds paid for my research assistants Crystal Zapanta, Lauren Pollini, Jenny Mar, Shane Kennedy, and Maddie Holiman—who all did the chores I don't like and cheerfully asked for more.

The Friday Writing Warriors have supported and sustained this work and one another for over four years, and each week has been a blessing. Thanks especially to Annick Wibben, Shawan Worsley, Karen Bouwer, Lois Lorenzen, Paula Birnbaum, and Marjolein Oele.

At the University of Nebraska Press: Thanks to Ladette Randolph, my first reader. To Kristen Rowley and Courtney Ochsner for their patience and attention. And to Heather Lundine for upholding the faith in good books.

On my journey through the world of oncology: I thank Dr. Alfredo Lopez, the very model of a doctor, and the spectacular women in my cancer support groups in both San Francisco and L.A. I hope this book will honor in some small way the memories of Ann, Anne, Miriam, Deb, Bonnie, Elizabeth, Julie, Christine, Jeniffer, and Lani as well as the courage, grace, and good humor of the rest of us.

In life: A bow and deep gratitude to my meditation teachers and fellow practitioners for their wisdom along the road.

Most deeply, I thank my sisters Tara and Shannon, who were there and still are; my daughters Kate and Erin, who humor and inspire me; and Frederick, who continues to surprise me with joy. *Namaste.*

Selected Bibliography

PRELUDE

Momaday, N. Scott. "A Divine Blindness." Reprinted in *Georgia Review* 4, no. 1 (Winter 2001–Spring 2002): 350–59.

————. *The Way to Rainy Mountain*. Albuquerque: University of New Mexico Press, 1969.

THE GOOD LAND

Homer. *The Odyssey*. Translated by Robert Fitzgerald. New York: Vintage Classics, 1990.

Starr, Kevin. *California: A History*. New York: Modern Library, 2005.

Stegner, Wallace. "The Sense of Place." In *Where the Bluebird Sings to the Lemonade Springs: Living and Writing in the West*, 199–206. New York: Random House, 1992.

AMAZING GRACE

Frazier, Ian. *The Great Plains*. New York: Penguin, 1989.

WICHITA VORTEX REDUX

Bader, Robert Smith. *Hayseeds, Moralizers, and Methodists: The Twentieth-Century Image of Kansas*. Lawrence: University of Kansas Press, 1988.

Eick, Gretchen Cassel. *Dissent in Wichita: The Civil Rights Movement in the Midwest 1954–72*. Urbana: University of Illinois Press, 2001.

Fonstad, Mark, William Pugatch, and Brandon Vogt. "Kansas Is Flatter than a Pancake." *Annals of Improbable Research*, May–June 2003, 16–18.

Ginsberg, Allen. "Wichita Vortex Sutra." In *Collected Poems 1947–1980*. New York: Harper and Row, 1984.

Greenough, Charles Pelham, III. "The Graphic Work of Birger

Sandzén." In *The Graphic Work of Birger Sandzén*. Lindsborg KS: The Birger Sandzén Memorial Foundation, 2001.

"Homespun Fun." *Sherman County Historical Society Newsletter* 7, no. 4 (May 1982): 4.

O'Connor, Pat. "Moody's Skidrow Beanery." Virtual Library. http://www.vlib.us/beats/oconnor.html.

Quietly Outspoken: Lester Raymer; An Exhibition. Lindsborg KS: Raymer Society, 1998. Published in conjunction with the exhibition shown at the Wichita Art Museum, September 20, 1998–January 10, 1999.

Scharnhorst, Gary. "Moodie [*sic*], My Dad, Allen Ginsberg, and Me: Reflections on Wichita and 'Wichita Vortex Sutra.'" *Midwest Quarterly* 45 (2004). http://www.questia.com/.

Walters, Ronald. "Standing Up in America's Heartland—1950's Civil Rights Movement in Wichita, Kansas." *American Visions* 8, no. 1 (February–March 1993): 20–23.

Whitman, Walt. *Leaves of Grass: The "Death-Bed" Edition*. New York: Modern Library, 2000.

KANSAS BECOMES ME

Benét, Stephen Vincent. *John Brown's Body*. Chicago: Ivan R. Dee, 1927.

John Brown of Kansas, 1855–1859. N.p.: Territorial Kansas Heritage Alliance, 2000.

Miner, H. Craig. *Wichita: The Early Years, 1865–80*. Lincoln: University of Nebraska Press, 1982.

Quarles, Benjamin. *Allies for Freedom & Blacks on John Brown*. Cambridge MA: Da Capo Press, 2001.

Sandoz, Mari. *The Buffalo Hunters: Story of the Hide Men*. New York: Hastings House, 1954.

Unrau, William E. *Indians of Kansas*. Topeka: Kansas State Historical Society, 1991.

SACRED BUNDLES, SECRET MAPS

Blake, Henry T. *Chronicles of New Haven Green*. New Haven CT: Tuttle, Morehouse, and Taylor Press, 1898.

Federal Writers' Project of the Work Projects Administration for the State of Kansas. *Kansas: A Guide to the Sunflower State*. New York: Viking Press, 1939.

Fowler, Loretta. *The Columbia Guide to American Indians of the Great Plains*. New York: Columbia University Press, 2003.

Good, Diane L. *Birds, Beads & Bells: Remote Sensing of a Pawnee Sacred Bundle*. Anthropological Series 15. Topeka: Kansas State Historical Society, 1989.

Kindscher, Kelly. *Edible Wild Plants of the Prairie: An Ethnobotanical Guide*. Lawrence: University of Kansas Press, 1987.

Weltfish, Gene. *The Lost Universe: Pawnee Life and Culture*. Lincoln: University of Nebraska Press, 1965.

Williamson, J. W. "The Battle of Massacre Canyon: The Unfortunate Ending of the Last Buffalo Hunt of the Pawnees." *Trenton (NE) Republican Leader*, 1922.

WHAT THE PRAIRIE TEACHES

Cather, Willa. *My Ántonia*. New York: Signet Classic, 1944.

Jackson, Wes. *Becoming Native to This Place*. Washington DC: Counterpoint Press, 1994.

———. *New Roots for Agriculture*. New edition. Lincoln: University of Nebraska Press, 1985.

MATFIELD GREEN

Berry, Wendell. "The Thought of Something Else." *Selected Poems of Wendell Berry*. New York: Counterpoint Press, 1998.

Calvino, Italo. *Invisible Cities*. Translated by William Weaver. New York: Harcourt Brace Jovanovich, 1972. Reprinted in 1974.

Scraping By in the Big Eighties
by Natalia Rachel Singer

In the Shadow of Memory
by Floyd Skloot

Secret Frequencies
A New York Education
by John Skoyles

Phantom Limb
by Janet Sternburg

Yellowstone Autumn
A Season of Discovery in a
Wondrous Land
by W. D. Wetherell

My Ruby Slippers
The Road Back to Kansas
Tracy Seeley

....

To order or obtain more
information on these
or other University of
Nebraska Press titles, visit
www.nebraskapress.unl.edu.